W. B. YEATS

William Butler Yeats *(1865–1939) is considered to be one of the greatest poets of the twentieth century. A writer of verse since his teenage years, it was the publishing of* The Wanderings of Oisin *(1889) that brought him his first favourable reviews and established a reputation that was to grow and grow.*

His early poems are distinguished by images from the legends of Celtic mythology and by a lyrical directness and wish to communicate with the Irish people. His involvement in Irish Nationalist politics, and his unrequited love for the revolutionary Maud Gonne, inspired the poetry of his middle years. His later work is bleaker, more elaborate in style and theory than his early work and heavily influenced by the symbolism of the occult.

Largely responsible for founding Dublin's Abbey Theatre, home of the Irish National Theatre Society established in 1901, Yeats wrote several fine plays that were performed there. He was made a senator of the Irish Free State in 1922 and received the Nobel Prize for Literature in 1923.

Author **David Ross** *has written an engaging and accessible biography of W.B. Yeats. Given the huge range of Yeats's interests – poetry, philosophy, history, mysticism and politics – and his eventful personal and public lives, Ross has deftly captured the spirit of the man and his work, relationships and beliefs.*

W. B. YEATS

David Ross

MERCIER PRESS

Published 2020 by Mercier Press, Cork, www.mercierpress.ie,
by arrangement with Geddes & Grosset, an imprint
of The Gresham Publishing Company Limited,
31, Six Harmony Row, Glasgow G51 3BA, Scotland.

Text by David Ross
Cover illustration by Maurice Mechan

ISBN 978-1-78117-775-4

Printed and bound in the EU

CONTENTS

Contents

CHAPTER ONE

CHILDHOOD OF A POET

Towards the close of a speech in the Senate of Ireland, in June 1925, William Butler Yeats spoke of the section of the Irish community from which he himself came:

'We against whom you have done this thing, are no petty people. We are one of the great stocks in Europe. We are the people of Burke; we are the people of Grattan; we are the people of Swift, the people of Emmet, the people of Parnell. We have created the most of the modern literature of this country. We have created the best of its political intelligence.'

Although he was making a general statement rather than describing his own personal ancestry, there is no doubting the pride and even arrogance lying behind those words. Yeats was conscious that the Protestant Irish had contributed greatly to their country's fame – to a greater degree, perhaps, than their numbers might suggest. Like many others emerging from that community, he had been a dedicated supporter of national independence: his Senate seat was in part the reward for his contribution. But he had come to appreciate the

unpalatable fact that within the greater liberty, the freedom of self-determination in Ireland, some lesser liberties
were going to fall and die. He was speaking against the
Divorce Bill, which was to outlaw civil divorce in Ireland
for many decades. For Yeats, who had not, since boyhood,
been a Christian, there were stronger and holier bonds
than marriage to bind individuals together. But he cher-
ished above all the individual's freedom to go his, or her,
own way. The passing of the anti-divorce legislation was
a defeat for him, a small defeat. But the speech against it
had been, in its own way, a brave action. In Yeats's view of
things, to win was good, but to be a hero was all-important.
And heroes are always, in the end, defeated.

In June 1925, Yeats was sixty years old. He was a public
man, and a famous one: by far Ireland's most renowned
living writer. In the previous year he had been awarded
the Nobel Prize for Literature. But the externals of success and position did not conceal the fact that he was
not a practical politician or a literary panjandrum. He
was a visionary. For more than forty years his life had
consisted of an intense inner dialogue, in which his intel-
lect and his personal feelings had striven to make sense
of the way in which he saw the world; and striven again
to express that way to others. At an age when many
men are ready to sit back from life, he was on the brink
of further crises, further discoveries, more insights; he
was also capable of rethinking and reshaping the way in
which he wrote, so as to give his thoughts their fullest
and most satisfying expression.

The life of William Yeats, from start to finish, was that of a poet. Everything else was incidental. He lived, thought, worked as a poet. He was fortunate, being a man who was not immune to considerations of money, social position and fame, that his poetry brought him all three. Nothing else would have done it for him.

That life began in Dublin, on June 13th, 1865. The house, now 5 Sandymount Avenue, is not a grand place, but poets have been born in worse houses, and, poetically speaking, into worse families. The house was rented by his father, John Butler Yeats. William was the first child born to John and his wife Susan. The Yeatses lived in Dublin because John Yeats was studying for the bar. In the Dublin of 1865, to become a barrister was to achieve a pleasingly comfortable level of social status and income. The capital of Ireland at that time had the status of a provincial British city. Since 1800 its parliament had been incorporated into the Westminster parliament of the United Kingdom of Great Britain and Ireland. Its official Church was a branch of the Church of England. Its never-abandoned national Church was emerging from a long period of deprivation and official attempts to uproot it entirely, to a grudging governmental acceptance that ensured it kept its policies to the most conservative. London was the focus for politics and the (mostly Protestant) aristocracy. The law, and its practice and practitioners, was almost the only secular relic of Dublin's capital status.

But J.B. Yeats, to the consternation of his wife and

in-laws, was to throw over his no-doubt bright and prosperous future as a Dublin advocate. He had been called to the bar (i.e. become a junior barrister) and worked for a notable figure, Isaac Butt, leader of the Irish MPs at Westminster until Charles Stewart Parnell assumed the leadership. But he followed the law for hardly more than a year. When William was not yet two, and another child, Susan (known in the family as Lily), less than a year old, he abandoned his legal career to become an artist. Early in 1867 he enrolled as a student at Heatherley's Art School in London. The result was a divided, impecunious and uncomfortable life for his family. But as an example to his eldest son, even though William was far too young to appreciate it at the time, it was a crucial action.

It showed the young Yeats two things -- one was that a man could take a decisive step on behalf of his own artistic conscience and personal development, without too much concern as to the welfare of his family, even when he was the 'breadwinner'; secondly, and somewhat conversely to the first, that it was very desirable not to be short of money.

John B. Yeats, though a talented painter, never achieved real success. He tried portraits; he tried landscapes. He worked in London, Dublin and New York. But the finding of a style that was distinctively and convincingly his own always eluded him. His inability to complete a portrait commission became legendary. It was his youngest child, Jack, who would become a painter of high distinction. The elder Yeats's income as a painter was small, spasmodic and generally insufficient to meet the needs of a growing family. In addition to his fees as a painter, there was some family money. The Yeatses had owned property in Dublin and land in County Kildare. John Yeats's stewardship of this was not to benefit his children: mortgaging and poor management (he entrusted supervision of the tenancies to an uncle who committed suicide when threatened with bankruptcy) eventually reduced the income to a fraction of what it might have been.

William's mother, Susan, came from the prosperous Pollexfen merchant family of Sligo; there is no doubt that her husband's change of career was a shock and a source of anxious concern to her. To return to her parents' house with two babies, while John pursued his dream in London, was an admission of failure. For most of William's early life, there would be a polarity between father and mother, between London and Sligo, between city and country, between the voluble communication of intellectual ideas and a withdrawn, depressed attitude to life. But the mother also gave the slow, rich feed of an inheritance of folklore and story. In July 1867, Susan and the children went to live with John in a rented house at 23 Fitzroy Road, a recently developed district a little way north of Regent's Park. By 1870, the young family had increased with two more children, Elizabeth (known to the others as Lolly) and Robert (who died of an attack of croup at the age of three).

For the children there were many visits to Sligo. The Pollexfens were part-owners of a steamship company trading between Liverpool and the west of Ireland: the daughter and grandchildren of a Director were privileged passengers (by contrast the sailors were said to be hostile to J.B. Yeats, perhaps reflecting a prejudice of their managers). William Pollexfen, the grandfather, and whose name the boy bore, was a man who would always loom large in Yeats's imagination and memory; like many another impressionable child confronted with a high Victorian grandpa, he confused this stern, bearded, irate elderly figure with God.

The boy Willie, as he was always known to his family and intimate friends, was powerfully influenced by the times he spent in Sligo and its surrounding district. It was still a quiet country town, set amid fine scenery and facing outwards to the sea. His grandparents were important citizens, and their house, Merville, was a substantial place on the outskirts of the town, with its own stables and sixty acres of land. There were cousins who also came to stay for the summer, at a house out on Rosses Point; and Yeats relations in the area too. He could feel that this was where he belonged. The traditions and legends of an older Ireland were still preserved here, and among the servants his grandfather employed were many who could tell the boy stories that went back to the days of druids, of heroes, of proud queens and bards whose utterances were treated as prophecy.

Between 1872 and 1874, Susan returned with her

children to Sligo, a move brought about most probably
by the inability of J.B. Yeats to support them, but she was
also out of sympathy with his ambitions and disliked
his London friends. John Butler Yeats made numerous
visits. His lack of success as an artist did not appear
to reduce his confidence in other ways. Conscious of
the somewhat grander ancestry of the Yeatses to the
Pollexfens (a distant ancestor had ben a connection of the
Duke of Ormond, hence the preservation of the Butler
name within the family), he was as ready to patronize
their mercantile status as they were to deplore his indifference to financial success. He took a close interest in
the development of his eldest son, all the more perhaps
because of their frequent separations. John Butler
Yeats, the artist who had put his own vocation ahead of
worldly success, was not likely to share the ambitions
of the Pollexfens for his son. Their view of a successful
future was firmly based on the 'Three Rs'; all of which
the boy was slow to acquire, despite the efforts of his
aunts. His father was more concerned with such matters
as the boy's acquisition of taste and judgement. But he
had no scheme of education for Willie. On his sum-
mertime visits he would read to the boy from chosen
works, concentrating especially on the highly dramatic
moments of Lord Macaulay's *Lays of Ancient Rome*, or Sir
Walter Scott's poems and novels. He had some reasons
for concern. Willie seemed to be a dreamy, introspective
boy, slow to learn, not interested in the sort of practical
matters that were the daily concern of the Pollexfens and

Middletons. During this Sligo phase of his childhood, he
was told of the voice of conscience; the phrase troubled
him as he had never heard such a voice. Then one day
he heard a voice within him whisper: 'What a tease you
are'. From then on, he recorded, the voice came to him
in moments of crisis: 'It does not tell me what to do, but
often reproves me'. His relations, who looked on the
artist's son as a chip off the old block, did not hesitate
to criticise him or try to bring him into line with their
own notions of what a boy should be doing. Though
John Yeats would often lose patience with Willie, both
as a boy and a man, he appears to have sensed from an
early stage that the boy had unusual qualities of imagination and feeling. Unlike the conventional expectation
of a Victorian parent's behaviour he did not attempt to
eradicate these qualities. After all, he himself was an artist.

Late in 1874, Susan and the children rejoined John in
London, to live in a house they had taken in the North
End Road, West London; then a newish district but
already assuming the shabbiness of the capital's hastily
run-up Victorian streets. A sixth child was born there,
in August 1875, but died before she was a year old. Like
most children of his era, the young Yeats was to experience the closeness and arbitrary snatchings of death from
an early age.

In 1876, with his wife and children again back in Sligo,
J.B. Yeats took lodgings at Burnham Beeches, in Buck-
inghamshire, England, and brought Willie, by now aged
eleven, over to stay with him. At the start of 1877,

family life in West London resumed once again, and
Willie was sent to Godolphin School in Hammersmith
(now Godolphin and Latymer, a girls-only school). He
was to spend four years here, most of the time feeling
himself to be an outsider. His life to this point had little resemblance to that of the West London schoolboys
who were his class-mates. The teaching at the school
was dull and unimaginative. In the playground he was
often mocked for his Irish speech and his stand-offish
ways. He learned to develop a tough outer skin and to
stand up to bullying. At home (the family moved a little
further west to the arty Bedford Park area of Chiswick
when Willie was thirteen), he was the young king. His
attitude to his two sisters, Lily and Lolly, would always
be that of the big brother – self-assertive, demanding,
critical, somewhat patronizing. His position was perhaps
enhanced when the youngest surviving child of the
Yeatses, Jack, was sent at the age of seven to Sligo to live
with his grandparents. J.B. Yeats could not support his
growing children. But Willie was now the only boy in
the household. He was a focus for the attention of two
very different people. John Yeats, sociable, talkative, full
of questions and demands; in touch with literary and
artistic culture; and Susan Yeats, quiet, intense, brooding; caring more for old stories than new ones. With
the ready irritation of the clinically depressed, she had
little patience for her son. The perceptive, imaginative
child could see in his own parents the masks and fronts
that people wear. Behind his father's ebullience was the

striving for success and a growing sense of failure. Other men were establishing names and fortunes for themselves as painters, including fellow-Irishmen like Lavery and Orpen. In later years, John Butler Yeats, increasingly aware of his own failure, would remove himself from both London and Dublin to watch his sons' success from the haven of New York. Behind his mother's reserve and quietness was the sense that her marriage, in the eyes of her own family, was a poor one. And she was an exile, living in a little rented house, on a scanty and irregular income, in a vast city and a strange country, while her heart yearned for Sligo. But her husband also saw a family tendency of the Pollexfens to mental instability, and feared that his children might inherit it.

John Butler Yeats was a free-thinker whose rational view of life, heavily influenced by his reading of the English philosopher John Stuart Mill, was not sympathetic to organized religion or to mysticism of any kind. But Susan took her children to church and saw to it that they were taught the elements of Christianity. At the age of fifteen, Willie was confirmed as a communicant of the Church of England. But in the middle of 1881, the London life came to an end. Disillusioned with his attempts to establish himself in England, J.B. Yeats decided to return to Ireland. There would be a fresh beginning. The family moved to Dublin, where he rented a studio. At the age of sixteen, no longer a child, Willie Yeats discovered the city of which one day he would become the most celebrated inhabitant.

None of that future fame was apparent in 1881, and the family lived outside the city, at Howth, then a fishing village, although already some Dubliners commuted into the city by means of the train. It was a happy time, especially for Yeats's mother, who enjoyed talking to the fishermen's wives. Willie found the Hill of Howth and its cliffs a congenial place to develop his interest in geology and also in moths and butterflies. These were fashionable pursuits for a young intellectual, linked as they were with the great scientific revelations of the nineteenth century, the age and basic structure of the earth; and the evolution of species. It was also a fine place for solitary rambles in romantic mode, in the manner of Shelley's idealized poet in 'Alastor', or Byron's Manfred. His father's enthusiasm and his own responsiveness had him in the full grip of these 'Romantic' poets, who, apart from their often highly indistinct ideas, also were masters of versification and metre.

> 'I soon chose Alastor for my chief of men and longed to share his melancholy, and maybe at last to disappear from everyone's sight as he disappeared drifting in a boat along some slow-moving river between great trees.'
> (*Autobiographies*)

Meanwhile, he went every weekday into Dublin with his father. They breakfasted together in the artist's studio. Commissions were not so overwhelming that John Yeats did not have ample time to talk to his son.

Whatever the shortcomings of his early education, there was now no doubt of the intelligence and largeness of mind of the adolescent Yeats. The subjects which he and his father discussed, or on which his father declaimed, were chiefly art and literature, along with the rational and anti-religious philosophical views of contemporary thinkers like Herbert Spencer. John Butler Yeats renewed his circle of Dublin friends from the law, the arts and the colleges, and there were often visitors at the breakfast table. These sessions were very important in the boy's mental development. In later life Yeats wrote:

'I have tried to create standards, to do and say those things that accident made possible to me, the accident being I suppose in the main my father's studio.'

(*Letter to Arthur Power, June 1935*)

From these memorable breakfasts Willie then went on to school, at the Erasmus Smith High School in Harcourt Street, a dull institution, whose teachings were often subverted by the impatient father. Mundane subjects like Geometry or Geography were of little account to the artist, who believed that a cultured person could pick up all he required from his own reading. Yeats's father believed in 'training for the mind'; in effect, this amounted to little more than the transmission to his son of his own attitudes and opinions. The inevitable tension between the school's dreary insistence on learning the standard range of subjects, and his father's airy dismissiveness of this, made Willie extremely unhappy, or contributed to feelings of unhappiness that he already had. The almost unavoidable guilts of Victorian youth: the problems and urgings of sexual development; the beginnings of doubt about religion as taught, the awareness of parental tensions and the consequent conflict of loyalties, all added to his burden, The boy did not shine at Erasmus Smith any more than he had at Godolphin, but he began to make friends.

He was also evolving a kind of personal style. In a memoir in the school's magazine, *The Erasmian,* June 1939, a schoolfellow, W.K. Magee, recalled him as 'a kind of super-boy who enjoyed an enviable immunity from the various ignominies of school discipline'. The advanced views Willie picked up at the paternal breakfasts were recounted to the impressed and slightly scandalized ears of his schoolmates. Erasmus Smith was of course a Protestant school but it is clear that the attitudes of its staff were conservative in all respects. Its Christianity was traditional, its politics Unionist, its focus not on the green country to the west but on the imperial nation unseen across the sea to the east. Another old classmate, Dr F.R. Montgomery Hitchcock, remembered that 'when we were ordered to write English verse, his was always astounding to us'. Poetry, or at least the making of verses, had already begun. So had the poetic persona.

To be a poet in Dublin was not to be an original. In

1881, aged twenty-seven, Oscar Wilde published his first volume of poetry, 'Patience'. Though no longer a resident of Dublin, his career was observed with great interest by the city's literary and social circle. Shocking but delicious stories of his utterances and behaviour were already drifting back across the Irish Sea. While it is not likely that young Yeats took the older poet as a conscious role-model, he felt that the poet must be revealed in his life as well as in his verses. His poetic pose did not go down well with all his contemporaries. Some felt it displayed affectation and concealed arrogance, and one, who remained anonymous, writing in 1912 when Yeats was still a figure of some controversy, described it as 'repellent' (*T.P.'s Weekly*, June 1912). Yeats himself was to put the blame on seeing the actor Henry Irving perform in Shakespeare's 'Hamlet': 'Years afterwards I walked the Dublin streets when nobody was looking, or nobody that I knew, with that strut Gordon Craig has compared to a movement in dance, and made the character I created speak with his brooding, broken wildness.' Had Yeats not found his model in Irving, he would surely have invented it. As it was, it is easy to understand how the character of Hamlet, caught in a tragic gulf between the commands of a dead but still powerful father, and his ambivalence towards a living mother; full of an intense and bitter self-awareness; feeling the desirability of action without knowing how to go about it, all shaped into coherence by the actor's genius, could imprint itself deeply on an impressionable teenager.

He was not a sexually precocious youth, and records in his *Autobiography* how he discovered masturbation, to his own surprise, at the age of fifteen after swimming naked – as was the normal practice of the time – in the sea at Rosses Point in Sligo. His views of women veered from the fictive to the real after he met his first love, Laura Armstrong, who was staying at the time not far away from the Yeatses on the Hill of Howth. Laura was an unconventional girl for the era, who went out driving alone, wore no hat, and spoke to strange young men. She was also three years older than Willie and engaged to someone else, not that marriage with young Yeats was ever in question. The gawky, poetic schoolboy was forced to listen to her agonizings over her engagement, of the arguments and fights with her fiancé, while jealousy and desire burned within him. Of Laura he recorded that 'she woke me from the metallic sleep of science and set me writing my first play'.

If Laura was the muse, then it was due to the influence of John Butler Yeats, that the boy's first poetic efforts were largely dramatic. His first major poem, 'The Wanderings of Oisin', was still some years away, but it had many predecessors in which noble figures, destined to misunderstanding and death, confessed their feelings and expressed their raptures amid scenery of Alpine grandeur far removed from anything that Yeats had yet seen with his outward eyes.

The friendship with Laura resulted in a complete play, 'Time and the Witch Vivien', performed for friends in the drawing room of the house where Laura lived (it was the home of Judge Wright, who was also owner of the modest cottage rented by J. B. Yeats in Howth village).

It might have seemed that the way ahead was clear. William Yeats would become a poet. But in fact the way ahead was murky and obscure. Many teenage schoolboys moon around with poetic phrases in their minds, have coltish passions for older girls, even write some better-than-average verses, before the iron rails of a business career emerge from the mists. For Willie, the mists showed no sign of parting.

CHAPTER TWO

*E*MERGENCE OF A POET

As his final year at Erasmus Smith drifted towards its
undistinguished end, it was necessary for the young Yeats
to take up a career. His father's move back to Ireland
had not resulted in any change of fortune: his income
was still small and unpredictable. They had moved from
Howth to Terenure, where 10 Ashfield Terrace must have
seemed reminiscent of the grimy streets of West London
which the family had left with relief. Willie disliked it
intensely. Certainly it was no home for an Alastor, and
far in every way from the woods and furze of Howth,
where sometimes he had slept out at night in the castle
grounds.

The natural progression for young Yeats would have
been to enter Trinity College, the finishing school for
young men of the Protestant community. His father, his
grandfather and his great-grandfather on the Yeats side
were all graduates of Trinity; one of J.B. Yeats's closest
friends was Edward Dowden, the Professor of English
and biographer of Willie's hero-poet Shelley. But now
the slow learning and the neglect of basic subjects took
their toll. Convinced that he would not pass the entrance

examinations, Willie did not give Trinity the chance to refuse him. Instead he eventually enrolled, in autumn 1884, at the Metropolitan School of Art in Kildare Street. His two sisters had become students there a year before. It was not a career choice. Art seemed to be the family occupation, so he simply drifted with the current.

Internationally, it was an exciting time in art. In Paris, the traditional approach and style were under challenge from a new generation of artists. In London there was controversy. Four years had passed since John Ruskin had accused James McNeill Whistler of 'throwing a pot of paint in the face of the public' and the future of art was in debate. In Kildare Street, the certainties and practices of an earlier world reigned. Its teaching in the early years was a boring routine in which pupils copied geometrical shapes and classical forms. There was no interest in new developments. Willie Yeats had a talent for art, and won a drawing prize, but art did not possess him with the consuming drive of his young brother Jack. The claim on his energies lay elsewhere. Discipline at the art school was light, and he neglected his classes in favour of writing, and the pursuit of his growing interest in matters spiritual and occult. Another student there was George Russell, an Ulsterman, who was to become a celebrated writer and artist himself under his pseudonym of AE. An intensely spiritual and visionary person, he soon joined with Yeats and Yeats's school friend Charles Johnston in attempts to perceive and interpret a world beyond the physical one. They read poems to one another; on one occasion Yeats disturbed the Russell family by throwing stones at George's window in the middle of the night: he wanted to show him the completed version of a poem they had been discussing earlier.

In 1884 Laura Armstrong had finally married her fiancé and the long flirtation with Yeats had to end. For a time, there was no woman in his life to give focus to his whirling creative energies. Lack of money, and perhaps other factors, tied him to the family home in the much-loathed Terenure. The still centre of that family was the mother, about whom Yeats said very little in his autobiographical writings. Indifferent if not hostile to art and writing, brought up to believe that men were providers, and to expect a comfortable home, she was not only married to an unsuccessful artist but the mother of three art students. To see Willie apparently following the same road that John was so unprofitably treading must have accentuated his mother's depressive state. But she was not the sort to give vent to her feelings.

John Butler Yeats was not so reticent. It soon became clear to him that in a number of ways, his eldest son was charting out an independent course which had nothing directly to do with the paternal teachings or opinions. A hardy rationalist who had no time for mystic speculations, he saw his son become more and more obsessed by a belief in a spiritual – though far from conventionally religious – other-world. A convinced supporter of Irish-British unionism, though supportive of 'Home Rule', he saw his son develop into an active adherent of the Irish independence movement. These were tendencies not only to be deplored but to be countered. Arguments between father and son often became noisy and occasionally even violent. On one occasion J.B. Yeats pushed Willie so hard against a picture hanging on the wall that the glass broke against his head.

While neglecting his art studies in 1885, Yeats in that same year saw his name in print for the first time. He became acquainted with a busy young academic at Trinity, C.H. Oldham, founder of the new *Dublin University Review*. The second issue of the magazine contained two short lyrics by Yeats, 'Song of the Faeries', and 'Voices'. Future issues would publish in serial form a much more substantial poem, 'The Island of Statues'. Publication in the *Review* demonstrated the young poet's links with a political movement, The Young Ireland Society. Its founder was John O'Leary, who had just returned to Ireland after twenty years of imprisonment and enforced exile for suspected anti-Union revolutionary activities. O'Leary was a commanding and picturesque figure whose first remarks at the Society's inaugural meeting were:

'I have come back from exile with the same opinions and feelings I carried with me into prison.'

This charismatic man of action was to play an important part in Yeats's life, both as a kind of substitute father-figure for J.B. Yeats, and, something that John was unable to do, as a dynamic and generous agent in supporting Willie's literary work. O'Leary realized that

to bring about a change of political climate in Ireland
and to bring the people to a point where independence
was their prime concern, a war of ideas was necessary
as a parallel to political action. He was familiar with the
writings of the earlier 'Young Ireland' movement of the
nineteenth century. Young writers with a strong sense
of Irishness and the requisite political commitment were
to be sought out and encouraged. He introduced Yeats
to the work of poets such as Thomas Davis. Later on,
after Yeats had gained much political maturity, he was to
look back on O'Leary as an embodiment of 'Romantic
Ireland', something that by then was 'dead and gone; It's
with O'Leary in the grave'. But in 1885 it was a heady
time for a passionate-spirited young Irishman.

The feeling of political hope ran high. With Charles
Stewart Parnell at the head of a solid phalanx of Irish
MPs in the Westminster parliament, able to hold the balance of power, there was a belief that the affairs of the
country were about to change dramatically. Whether
the aspiration was merely for 'Home Rule' or for total
independence, it was possible to believe that its realization was just round the corner.

In joining Young Ireland, Yeats took a definite step into
the political arena. In the same year he was one of the
founders of the Dublin Hermetic Society. Thinking back
over his younger days, he was to write: 'I did not think
I could live without religion.' In this spiritual quest, he
was moving away from his father's rational and agnostic
attitude and coming closer to his Pollexfen relations. His

mother's sister Isabella had already sent him A.P. Sinnett's
book *Esoteric Buddhism*. The Sligo connection, with its
interest in legends, ghosts and fairies, found an echo in
the teachings now being brought back from the Far
East. Yeats was already aware of the work of Madame
Blavatsky, founder of the Theosophy movement, whose
book *Isis Unveiled* had been published in 1877. Orthodox Christianity, still trying to come to terms with, or
to evade, the implacable messages of Darwinism and
the new geology, was at a low ebb. This was particularly
true of Protestantism. The Anglican Church, in which
Willie had been brought up, had seen the defections to
Roman Catholicism of such leading lights as John Henry
Newman and Henry Edward Manning, and was fighting
dissension within its own ranks at the other end of the
spectrum, where some vicars were tending to become little
more than theists in the face of the onslaught of scientific
ideas. Yeats had left science behind with his schoolboy's
butterfly net. His mind craved a wider understanding of
the significance of life. Like the explorer of a maze, he
was willing to try any number of entrances, aware they
might be false, or lead into danger, because of his profound
and instinctive assurance that if only the centre could be
reached, there would be a great and joyous revelation.

With its own mysteries and sense of celebration, its
ancient prestige, its costumes and its rituals; and not least
its central place in the historic life of the Irish people,
it is perhaps surprising that Catholicism appears to have
possessed little appeal to W.B. Yeats. Perhaps to 'go over'

would have seemed too great an apostasy against those sturdy Anglican ancestors mentioned in several of his poems. To Yeats, however, it was also a matter of class and tradition; the Anglican tradition being aristocratic and intellectual, and that of Catholicism populist and ill-taught. Also, to a well-informed and free-thinking young man, the church of Cardinal Cullen and Pope Pius IX would not have seemed a haven so much as a dead end. Politically conservative, authoritarian in style, inimical to new ideas, its appeal was to a soul that abjured questions and sought submission. Yeats's soul, ardent with questioning, wanted to soar.

By one of literature's coincidences which prompt speculation on what might have been, Dublin at that time housed a Catholic poet whose lyrical and spiritual intensity could rise to match that of the mature Yeats himself. Gerald Manley Hopkins, Jesuit priest, academic and poet, had been sent by his superiors to teach in University College, Dublin. But Hopkins did not seek to publish his work, and his poetry was scarcely known outside a narrow circle. He had read some of Yeats's earliest published verse, and made some mildly disparaging remarks, in a letter to Coventry Patmore, about the prentice poem 'The Two Titans', published in the *Review*, though he conceded it was 'still containing fine lines and vivid imagery'. The two never met, and Yeats in later life said he hated Hopkins's poetry.

Yeats was however making valuable friends. In early 1885 C.H. Oldham introduced him to Katharine Tynan, then twenty-four, a young writer of independent mind and spirit who had just brought out her own first collection of poems. She and Yeats formed a close literary friendship; recording her first impression of him, she wrote that he was 'beautiful to look at, with his dark face, its touch of vivid colouring, the night black hair, the eager dark eyes'. Sharing his political views, eager to discuss the technicalities as well as the subject-matter of poetry, intrigued by his oddities, Katharine Tynan became a vital confidante to the young poet.

Joining another new institution helped him to maintain a dialogue with his father. John and Willie both became members of the Contemporary Club, another brain-child of Oldham's, intended to provide a forum in which Dublin's intellectuals, of all shades of opinion, could meet and talk; but inevitably it attracted a larger proportion of those with nationalist sympathies. Douglas Hyde, John F.C. Taylor and John O'Leary were among the members. Formal debates were regular and vehement. To a poor or unconfident speaker, to be open to attack from such accomplished and forceful advocates as Taylor was an unnerving prospect. Willie, who would wander the countryside declaiming poems in the rain, or looking for spirits in the hills, or whimsically try to mesmerize the Tynan hens, might have seemed easy meat. But he proved to be a tough debater. His command of language did not desert him in speech, and his pose, knowing, arrogant, indifferent, served both to irritate his opponents and protect himself.

He was not a bland young man, nor a conventional one, nor a shy one. Where he thought he could find guidance, he asked. When the Indian theosophist Mohini Chatterjee came to speak to the Contemporary Club, Yeats engaged him in conversation. He asked if he should pray. The visitor replied that he should not. He offered Yeats a sort of mantra to say to himself every night:

> 'I have been a king,
> I have been a slave,
> Nor is there anything,
> Fool, rascal, knave,
> That I have not been.'

This motto of reincarnation had great appeal to the mind of Yeats, nourishing, or flourishing in, the poetic sensibility that would create the different personas of Michael Robartes, Red Hanrahan, Owen Aherne and Crazy Jane. Like every other experience, he would store this one up, to be used later in contexts hardly yet imagined.

Still at a deeply impressionable stage, Yeats attended his first Spiritualist séance, with Katharine Tynan, in January 1888. The effect was astounding and unsettling. He began to twitch and shake; then was thrown backward against a wall, as by some unseen force. In alarm, he tried to pray but instead shouted out the opening lines of Milton's 'Paradise Lost'. Although the event helped to convince him of the realities of spirit powers, he did not attend a séance again until he felt more able to manage his own reactions.

By the end of 1886, two of the three strands of the young Yeats's poetic motor had been fully energized: Ireland, and the spirit world; the third remained for the time being passive. His thoughts were by no means fully organized or his visions coherent. But he was already a person of some note in Dublin, not simply the son of John B. Yeats. In a substantial essay on the recently dead poet Sir Samuel Ferguson, published in the *Dublin University Review,* he brought together his political and literary views in a sharp attack on official literary criticism, as personified by his father's old friend Professor Dowden. He associated the neglect of Irish writing and culture with 'the shoddy society of "West Britonism" ', and in a high-flown reference to his own state of mind appealed to young men whom 'the emotion of Patriotism has lifted into that world of selfless passion in which heroic deeds are possible and heroic poetry credible'. His dream was of 'a national literature that made Ireland beautiful in the memory, and yet had been freed from provincialism by an exacting criticism, a European pose' (*Autobiographies*). Reading Ferguson, and also the works of Standish O'Grady (1846–1928) together with his recollections of the orally told folktales of Sligo, helped him to form a distinctive and Irish voice that escaped from the oppressive influence of the great English poets. For Yeats could look at contemporary Irish poets, and for all his loyalty, realize they were pioneers rather than great masters. It was probably also in this year that he was recruited into the Irish Republican Brotherhood, a secret society whose political aim was clear in its title. There was a considerable overlap in membership between this body and officially acceptable organizations like Young Ireland. It seems unlikely that Yeats actually took the oath of membership. If he did, the fact was not picked up by the intelligence network of Dublin Castle, or Yeats would not have later been the recipient of a British state pension (he did feature in a police report in 1899 as 'a literary enthusiast, more or less a revolutionary, and an associate of Dr Mark Ryan' – the implication is 'harmless').

But his lack of an independently rooted life, and his continuing financial dependence, dragged him away from Dublin. The restless John Butler Yeats had decided that his Irish sojourn was a failure. He determined to move back to London, and in early 1887, with his family in reluctant attendance, returned once again to the imperial capital and took up residence in an 'old and dirty and dank and noisy' house at 58 Eardley Crescent, near Earls Court. The nearby Exhibition Arena made it a brash, crowded place. The narrow pavements, the throngs of working-class Londoners, did not make a happy milieu for the young poet with his half-unconscious 'Hamlet' walk and his habit of chanting verse, his own or others', as he went along.

In London, homesick and cut off from his friends, Willie did not attempt to resume his art studies. Lit-

erature was his vocation, and he knew it. A long poem
was forming in his imagination. Meanwhile, he had to
try to contribute to the family's small income. In this
he was greatly helped by a Contemporary Club connection. William Morris, the poet, Socialist, and apostle
of the Arts and Crafts movement, had come to Dublin
to talk to the Contemporaries, and Willie had met
him. Now Yeats reintroduced himself to the great man
and was well-received. Morris took a keen interest in
the 'Irish Question' but also in the old poetry of Ireland,
whose hero-figures and colourful mythology appealed
to his own vision of a medieval world unspoiled by
machinery and mass-production. Others in the Morris
circle shared these interests. One was Ernest Rhys, at
the start of a long career as an editor of classic texts. He
also shared Yeats's enthusiasm for the occult, but on a
more practical level he commissioned him to compile
a collection of *Irish Fairy Tales*, to be published by the
Walter Scott Company of Newcastle, an early operator
in the field of 'bargain books'.

Rhys's commission enabled Yeats to return to Ireland
for a research trip, with a free voyage on a Pollexfen ship
from Liverpool to Sligo. He left London in mid-August
1887 and did not return until early in 1888. By that
time he had not completed his collection of fairy stories,
but had finished the long poem on which he had been
brooding; in that rich air it became his first priority.

At Sligo he stayed first with his uncle George, then
with his grandparents. 'The very feel of the Sligo

earth puts me in good spirits' he wrote to Katharine
Tynan, who was urging him to come across to stay at
Clondalkin. Not until the narrative poem, 'The Wanderings of Oisin', was complete, in November, did he leave
Sligo. He stayed for some weeks at Clondalkin, and also
for a time with the O'Learys in Dublin. John O'Leary
was preparing an anthology, *Poems and Ballads of Young
Ireland,* with work by Yeats and Katharine Tynan, as well
as numerous others. O'Leary was enthusiastic about
'The Wanderings of Oisin', and proposed to set up a
subscription scheme of advance orders to enable it to be
published together with other poems by Yeats.

The news from England had been bad. Shortly before
Christmas, Susan Yeats suffered a slight stroke. Lily too
had been ill, and both women went to stay with Susan's
sister Elizabeth, married to a prosperous Yorkshire clergy-
man, to convalesce. But Susan fell victim to two further
and more severe strokes, which left her bedridden. Willie returned to a somewhat devastated family. But Jack
was now there too, attending art school. They moved
from the hated Earls Court house to Bedford Park in
Chiswick, to a more spacious house in a more pleasant
district, and one that was familiar to them from a decade
earlier. It also possessed more useful inhabitants for the
ambitious poet, men with publishing and literary connections; friends who could help.

Among these was William Ernest Henley (1849–
1903), a generation older than Yeats, who had been a
friend of Robert Louis Stevenson, till they had fallen

out. One of his legs had been amputated, due to illness, and he walked with a crutch. Henley specialized in helping younger writers, and had just taken over as editor of the *Scots* (to be renamed *National*) *Observer*. He gave Yeats work, and found him more elsewhere, and did not hesitate both to criticize and to 'improve' the younger man's work for publication. Yeats did not relish Henley's vulgar streak, nor his Imperialist politics, but, respecting his kindliness and his unremitting standards as an editor, was willing enough to be one of the numerous Henley disciples. At Henley's house he met Oscar Wilde. At William Morris's he met Bernard Shaw, another young man from Dublin who had sought the brighter lights of London. Yeats was an entertaining talker himself, but not a master of the kind of witty repartee in which Shaw and Wilde specialized; he was also more serious in spirit and regarded both these brilliant fellow-countrymen as somewhat shallow-minded. He nevertheless became Wilde's friend, enjoyed his hospitality, and was one who did not desert the playwright when his star so catastrophically fell; and remained in more sporadic but friendly contact with Shaw.

Some of Yeats's biographers have speculated that his familiarity with William Morris's household (his sister Lily also worked as an embroiderer for Morris's daughter May) taught him to recognize the value of, and put into practice, effective organization in the arts. Many enterprises were run from Kelmscott House, Morris's Thames-side home in Hammersmith, including print-

ing, textile and wallpaper design, theatre productions
and publications. Morris was an inveterate begetter of
projects. Whatever Yeats learned, he undoubtedly already
possessed the same instincts. He had already been a moving spirit of the Hermetic Club, and was to found other
bodies and organizations, as well as to lead a successful
national theatre company.

Literary earnings were low. Despite his poor eyesight,
Yeats also did some copying work, a source of low-paid
employment in these pre-electronic days. This activity
did not improve his spelling. Throughout his life he
was an inveterate bad speller; perhaps because of his
defective early education. Professor A.N. Jeffares, in his
biography of Yeats *W.B. Yeats, Man & Poet*, notes the
'classic' example: 'He puts sugger [sic] in his soup, in
his salad, in his vegetables, and then unexpectedly puts
salt on stewed pares [sic]'. The misspellings are usually
phonetically correct. A form of dyslexia has also been
suggested, but if it was, it certainly did not deter him
from either reading or writing.

The Yeatses could not afford new clothes or shoes. Their
genteel poverty, and Mrs Yeats's apathy, made it difficult
for them to entertain. Willie, working on Irish fairy tale
sources in the Reading Room of the British Museum,
would sometimes walk there from Chiswick to save the
fare. Rehearsing verses may have been pleasanter on
the pavements than in the sooty, smoky Underground,
still operated by steam engines. Delving into the early
sources of Irish folklore and legend enabled him to bring

together his Irish and psychic interests, but his being
in London, and his lack of knowledge of Gaelic, were
hindrances in the fairy tale business, and he made desperate appeals to his Young Ireland friend Douglas Hyde, a
Gaelic speaker who was collecting original stories from
the mouths of country people and translating them into
English. Hyde was generous with help and this enabled Yeats, with something of a scramble, to deliver the
manuscript on time. The book was dedicated to George
Russell, another invaluable source of contributions. Yeats
was pleased with the book, not least because the work of
compiling it had accumulated for him a great amount of
background knowledge which would be incorporated
in the poems he was already writing. It also helped to
convince him that there was a strong psychic element
long-established in the Irish character. These tales of ban-
shees, of the second sight, of visions and shape-changes,
of fairy-women and haunted knolls could not, he felt,
have arisen without some basis of fact.

Such thoughts fuelled his interest in the spiritual
world. At this time Yeats also met someone in whom he
had long been interested – Helena Petrovna Blavatsky,
whose house in the Holland Park area was a centre for
the many people captivated by her theosophical teachings and her own personal magnetism. The Theosophical
Society had been launched in 1875, in New York, by
Madame Blavatsky and Henry Olcott. She was of Rus-
sian origin, and strongly attracted to the mystic teachings
of Hindu and Buddhist wisdom. The principal aspect of

her cult was its view of life as a series of reincarnations of the human soul. These reincarnations ideally formed a progression through an unseen but structured universe involving a chain of seven planets. Spiritual powers presided over and guided this progression: an enlightened student might make contact with these powers and gain a fuller understanding of their workings, which would in turn assist progress towards the state of Nirvana or perfection, when reincarnations would cease. An enthusiastic student, Yeats was admitted to the Esoteric Section of the Society, which used carefully prescribed rituals to refine its contact with the spiritual world.

Yeats's school friend from Erasmus Smith, Charles Johnson, was one of the habitués: he was in love with Madame's niece and later married her. Yeats's relationship with Madame Blavatsky began well. He was impressed by her personality, her knowledge, her hard work and attention to detail. He praised her to such friends as John O'Leary and even, on a visit of O'Leary's to London, brought the sceptical old man to meet the woman-mage (he described her as 'a good-natured old woman'). But ultimately, Yeats was not the sort of pupil she preferred. She had laboured to make Theosophy into a complete system, embracing, in her view, all religions, and so offering her followers all the spiritual life they should need. Theosophy had grown into a highly successful cult, despite the frequently expressed scepticism of outsiders. In the process she had become a wealthy woman. She knew how important it was to maintain unity and discipline within her organization. Someone like Willie Yeats, profoundly interested, inquiring, opinionated and unafraid to express himself, was not likely to be a contented fare-paying passenger in her vessel. He was completely convinced that there was indeed an unseen world with which contact could be made, but he was by no means certain that Theosophy had all the answers. Keen to explore all the possible means of reaching the truth, he was soon to rock the boat by bringing in notions with which his pilot had no sympathy, and by the end of 1890 he would be asked to leave the Esoteric Branch.

The Wanderings of Oisin and Other Poems was published in January 1889, his first volume of verse to appear. Apart from the title poem, there were thirty other poems. 'Oisin' (Ossian), a narrative poem, takes up an old tradition, that of the meeting between St Patrick, busy converting the Irish to Christianity, and Ossian, son of Finn and last of the legendary warriors of the Fianna, who had been a prisoner in the land of the Fairies for three hundred years, lured there by the beauty of his beloved Niamh. There is no real dialectic between the ancient bard and the man with the crozier and the brazen bell; Yeats's purpose was to frame the spiritual quest of Oisin as he narrates his experiences and discoveries. In all its three manifestations, the fairy world is a delusion; Oisin must return to the mortal world to realize himself, to die, and to move into a new existence. This is the first poem in which Yeats successfully fuses Ireland's mystic past with his own sense of an immanent spiritual world which governs our lives. But its symbols and esoteric references were not obtrusive to the general reader. Filled with melodic and beautiful lines and haunting, powerful images, it was an impressive announcement that Yeats the poet, at the age of twenty-three, had arrived.

'Oisin' was dedicated to Edwin J. Ellis, a friend of J.B. Yeats and collaborator with W.B. in a new venture. Ellis was a painter and poet, and, like Yeats, an admirer of the work of William Blake (1757–1827), whom they regarded as a precursor of such persons as Blavatsky. For almost four years they worked together on a three-volume edition of Blake's works, with annotations. Blake as a mystical poet had indeed gone further than Yeats would ever do, referring to his poems as literally inspired, and saying to a friend he might praise the work as he liked, 'for I am but the Secretary'. The authors, he believed, were angels.

CHAPTER THREE

'*H*AMMER YOUR THOUGHTS INTO UNITY'

The *Oisin* poems show how Yeats had successfully brought Ireland and mysticism together. Less than three weeks after their publication, in January 1889, the third great strand of his work was galvanized into life, when he fell, suddenly and completely, in love.

Like a spirit from Niamh's unearthly islands, beautiful, arrogant, teasing, intense, passionate, vulnerable yet unattainable, Maud Gonne appeared out of nowhere on the Yeats doorstep in London. Or rather, out of Dublin, from where she brought a letter of introduction from O'Leary's daughter Ellen.

Maud was a member of Young Ireland, her Irish nationalism all the more passionate because it was to her a country of adoption and choice. She was born in England in 1864, and her father was a well-off professional soldier who had been posted with his regiment to Dublin Castle. She had grown up as a daughter of the English Ascendancy. It was her experience of the poverty and exploitation of the Irish peasantry that fired her to turn her back on England and indeed to come to hate it. She was young, beautiful, rich and free, moving at her pleasure from Paris to Dublin to London. Both her parents were dead.

William Yeats was a year older, poor, living somewhat claustrophobically with an invalid mother, two sisters, his brother and his father. He was tall, over six feet, and gangling. Untidy black hair dangled over his brow. His clothes were shabby yet worn with a certain flamboyance, as if to say 'this is my choice, not my need'. Finding a kindred spirit, Maud, flouting convention, invited him to dine with her that evening. They dined together again every day of her nine-day visit to London. By the end of it he was captivated, and his painful awareness of their difference in circumstances did nothing to reduce the growing obsession he now felt.

They had talked of the theatre, especially of a new, intrinsically Irish theatre; Maud had aspirations as an actress. He now addressed himself to writing a play for her, 'The Countess Cathleen', on which he would work for two years. But thoughts of Maud infused his whole being.

Yeats was a very innocent, and in many respects naïve, young man. His adventures in reading, thought and the spirit realm had not been paralleled by adventures in real life. Still a virgin, he was sexually shy, and intensely disliked the robust, nudging sexual vulgarity and coarse private eroticism of Henley and some other of his English acquaintances. His view of women was idealized and ethereal and it was in this light that he saw Maud Gonne,

with the additional warlike lineaments of an Irish Joan of
Arc, for Maud had no reservations about using violence
for political ends. He was completely unaware that Maud
had other dimensions in her life. She had talked darkly
of her political involvements in France. The populist,
semi-revolutionary party headed by General Boulanger
had attracted her, but she had also become the mistress
of an ambitious political journalist, of anarchist inclina-
tions, then in Boulanger's entourage, Lucien Millevoye.

Although they corresponded, he did not see her again
until the middle of 1891, when they were in Dublin
at the same time. Maud looked different then, pale,
bonier, subdued, lacking the vivacity he remembered so
clearly. Yeats had to leave to stay with Charles Johnson in
County Down, but a letter from Maud, not for the only
time, made him change his plans suddenly and return to
Dublin. Her letter had told him of a dream, in which he
and she were brother and sister, sold as slaves at the edge
of the great Arabian Desert. Abruptly, he asked her to
marry him. Maud replied that it was impossible, and in
a phrase he would bitterly remember, 'she would never
marry'. But she asked – not as the conventional sop to
the refused suitor – if they could still be friends. They
met every day and he read to her from the still unfin-
ished 'Countess Cathleen'. Again with mentions of
secret political intrigues, she left Dublin suddenly for
Paris. What had drawn her back was the illness of her
infant son, who had contracted meningitis. A few days
after her return, the baby died.

The obsession with Maud Gonne did not distract him from his other pursuits; rather Maud, or the thought of her, was made integral with them. While still a member of Madame Blavatsky's Esoteric Branch, he had, by the kind of coincidence which he believed to be spirit-led, met another teacher and found another way into the unseen universe. A fellow-researcher in the Reading Room of the British Museum was the imposing MacGregor Mathers (Samuel Liddell Mathers, 1854–1918), with whom Yeats struck up an acquaint-ance. They immediately found a common interest in Celtic mysticism. Mathers was one of the leaders of an organization called the Hermetic Order of the Golden Dawn. More exclusive than the Theosophical Society, as the 'hermetic' in its name suggests, its rituals and ideas were based more on medieval tradition, borrowing from the gnostic writings of the Jews, the Kabbalah, from Free-masonry, and from the quasi-Catholic mystic tradition of Rosicrucianism, with its emphasis on the sacrificial existence of Christ. The Order was elaborately organ-ized, with costumes and props such as swords, candles, incense, crosses and medallions. Unlike the Theosophists, the initiates of the Golden Dawn believed they could ex-ercise some control over the material world; their beliefs took them an exciting step closer to 'black magic'. As Yeats wrote in 1901:

'I cannot now think symbols less than the greatest of all powers whether they are used consciously by the masters of magic, or half-consciously by their successors, the poet, the musician and the artist . . . Whatever the passions of men have gathered about, becomes a symbol in the great memory, and in the hands of him who has the secret it is a worker of wonders, a caller-up of angels or of devils.'

In 1890 Yeats was admitted to the Order. With typical enthusiasm he embraced it and began trying out its mystic symbols upon his friends. Placing an intricate medallion on their brows, he would ask them to tell him what vision rose into their minds. One of his associates in all this was the Scottish writer William Sharp, the most thoroughgoing of all Celtic mystics. Mathers believed himself to be the reincarnation of a Highland chief, but Sharp had a complete, living alternative persona as Fiona MacLeod, the Celtic woman poet and novelist. Whether through ignorance of this, or through a delicate recognition of it, Yeats for some years corresponded with 'Fiona' in a manner which implied no awareness of her co-existence in the stout physical frame of his friend Sharp.

Central among the many symbols used by the Golden Dawn was the Rose, fraught with so many powerful associations – blood, pain, passion, intoxicating scent, the beauty, the thorns . . . Yeats was writing poems which used the symbol of the Rose to express his love for Maud:

> 'If Michael, leader of God's host
> When Heaven and Hell are met,
> Looked down on you from Heaven's door-post

He would his deeds forget.'
('The Rose of Peace')

He stayed on in Dublin, borrowing money from the helpful John O'Leary and renewing his friendship with George Russell. He was still in Dublin when Ireland was shocked by the death of Parnell in October of 1891. Maud came back to Dublin on the same ship that carried Parnell's coffin; her sombre black was taken to be mourning for the great 'lost leader'. She had written to tell Yeats that she was grieving for the death of a child whom she had adopted. Her distress and guilt were clear, and Yeats saw in them the presence of a troubling spirit which should be exorcized. Using techniques he had learned from MacGregor Mathers in the Order of the Golden Dawn, he brought out the spirit, a lady in grey: 'It was a past personality of hers now seeking to be reunited with her.' Maud found the experience a salutary one. She was interested to learn more of the Golden Dawn, and Yeats was pleased to make this a bond between them, hoping as ever that it would result in reciprocation of his love for her. They returned to London, Maud to stay with her sister, Yeats back to his family in Chiswick. He presented her with the 'Rose' poems, and, just before returning to Paris, she was initiated into the rites of the Golden Dawn.

The death of Parnell and the collapse of the Irish cause in the House of Commons made it clear that neither Home Rule nor national independence were waiting round the corner. John O'Leary and his followers did not give up the cultural struggle. Yeats played a vigorous part. He worked hard to help found Irish Literary Societies in London and in Dublin. This latter in particular was a national body, very different in scale and nature from the smaller groups he had known or helped start, and he found his own ideas and ambitions in danger of being left on the shelf by the superior organizing capacity of men like T.W. Rolleston. Maud, coming and going from Paris, took charge of an ambitious plan to open libraries and reading rooms throughout the country, where people who could not afford to buy books would be able to read Irish books rather than the commercial output of London publishers. Complementing this was a scheme to publish the necessary Irish books. Yeats's bid to be the arbiter of choice for this list, or at least one of them, was frustrated. His old Contemporary Club opponent, J.F. Taylor, derisively blocked Yeats's wish, branding him as a vain poetaster and a member of a self-regarding clique. Rolleston and Sir Charles Gavan Duffy, the veteran nationalist and author of Young Ireland, who considered himself to be Ireland's pre-eminent man of letters, began 'official' negotiations with the London publisher Fisher Unwin, with whom Yeats had already broached the notion. The eminent and elderly Gavan Duffy eventually became the principal selector of texts, to Yeats's rage, which was compounded by the fact that Maud Gonne had failed to back him on what he had come to consider a vital issue. The whole affair taught

Yeats lessons which he never forgot, and which were to influence the way in which he ran the Abbey Theatre.

With a second volume of poems published in summer 1892, under the title *The Countess Cathleen and Various Legends and Lyrics*, Yeats had anticipated a greater degree of recognition as a serious Irish poet. By now, this was definitely his view of himself, but his estimation, true as it was, ran somewhat ahead of that of many critics, who felt that he was setting himself up too high when he announced:

> 'Nor may I less be counted one
> With Davis, Mangan, Ferguson,
> Because to him that ponders well
> My rhymes more than their rhyming tell
> Of the dim wisdoms old and deep,
> That God gives unto man in sleep.'
> ('To Ireland in the Coming Times')

– the last three lines of the quotation were later revised. He was trying to make a specific point about his own writing, but it made him look simply like one who bragged that he was a better poet than the established masters. The sin of pride is a heinous one in Ireland, and Yeats might have fared worse than he did. But the merit of the poems was undeniable. 'The Countess Kathleen', a dramatic poem written for Maud Gonne, had a single performance in 1892, without Maud, to establish its copyright. Its story, of a mythical Irish countess who sells her pure and virginal soul to the devil in order to save her people from dying of starvation, links Maud's political activism to the still-smouldering national memory of the Great Hunger of 1848-52, and incorporates her would-be lover's lofty view of her sexual nature. It has some beautiful lines. But the poems in the collection include 'The Lake Isle of Innisfree' and 'When You Are Old'. As is often the way with the publication of immortal lyrics, these were not proclaimed from the rooftops as works of genius. They were respected, but they were of their time, and not yet perceptible as also being beyond their time. 'The Lake Isle of Innisfree' was the first poem that Yeats felt truly his own, and he traced its origins to his discontent with London, and his nostalgia for the Sligo countryside, where the island of the title lies in Lough Gill; the idea of the poem prompted by his reading of Thoreau's 'Walden', its imagery by his seeing a wooden ball balanced on a jet of water in a shop window; and by the osier-covered Chiswick Eyot, on the Thames near his home. Some of the poems in the collection show the poet swinging between points of influence: he borrowed the metre and manner of the English poet A.C. Swinburne for the quickly written 'The White Birds', when Maud had asked for a poem on the seagulls they saw at Howth; and there is an unassimilated quality to a 'modern' Irish poem like 'The Ballad of Father Gilligan', which might have been written by any lesser poet, whereas the 'old' Irish poem 'Cuchulain's Fight With the Sea' – the first of many poems about the tragic hero of legend – is far more Yeatsian. The

volume also contains four of the 'Rose' poems, which
are the first to integrate his feelings for Ireland, for the
spiritual world, and for his beloved. Throughout his life,
much of Yeats's thought revolved around the concept
of unity. Oneness was a spiritual quality, perhaps the
ultimate spiritual quality, in which all being is fused in a
transcendent perfection. In a very different way, but just
as seriously, he was striving towards a generalized 'Theory
of Everything' just like twentieth-century particle physi-
cists. But there were other, more mundane unities, no less
desirable in their modest way. One of these was the unity
of his own thoughts. Yeats recalled how in his early twenties, the insistent phrase rose in his mind: 'Hammer your
thoughts into unity.' The 'Rose' poems show this dictum
being put into effect:

> Come near, come near, come near – Ah, leave me still
> A little space for the rose-breath to fill!
> Lest I no more hear common things that crave . . .
> But seek alone to hear the strange things said
> By God to the bright hearts of those long dead,
> And learn to chaunt a tongue men do not know.
> Come near; I would, before my time to go,
> Sing of old Eire and the ancient ways:
> Red Rose, proud Rose, sad Rose of all my days.
> ('To the Rose Upon the Rood of Time', 1892)

    – almost every significant element in Yeats's thought
is present in this invocation.

Over in Sligo, the older generation was fading fast. That winter (1892), Yeats's Pollexfen grandparents died. He drew closer to his uncle George, who for all his horsiness and brusque manner, had a considerable interest in the occult, acquired from his involvement with Freemasonry, which his nephew helped to inflame, bringing him into the Golden Dawn. George also provided accommodation and occasional modest loans. One of their experiences was to summon up a fairy queen who, according to Yeats, not only told them about the economy of the fairy kingdom but also wrote a message in the sand to warn them against probing too far (letter from Yeats to Richard le Gallienne). Yeats was also fascinated by George Pollexfen's old servant Mary Battle, who saw fairy folk and was gifted, or afflicted, with the Second Sight. Stays with his uncle were not so much holidays as explorations of another facet of the occult, with long discussions on astrology and the tarot cards.

Yeats's life was settling into a pattern, albeit full of discordant patches. He was often in Ireland, in Dublin, or, if hard up, with Uncle George in Sligo. Whether in Ireland or in London, there were always several projects under way. He was working very hard, so hard that he became ill in 1890 and a doctor diagnosed heart trouble and ordered him to take more rest. In 1893 his collaboration with Ellis, which had become rather tedious, finally ended with the publication of their annotated Blake. This had a useful by-product in a commission to Yeats alone to edit an anthology of Blake's lyrical poems; and same publishers commissioned from him, under the evocative title *The Celtic Twilight,* a collection of folklore which he had also published piecemeal in Henley's *National Observer.* There were also the affairs of the Literary Societies, especially the Irish one, in whose affairs he by no means always got his own way. The Literary Society produced a vital offshoot in Douglas Hyde's Gaelic League, which reached further into the popular consciousness and was to have more political effect than its parent society. Yeats repaid his debt to Douglas Hyde by finding a London publisher for his translations of 'Songs of Connaught'. He was also writing poems influenced by his enduring and unsatisfied passion for Maud Gonne. He wrote her letters, and corresponded also with many others, depending on which side of the Irish Sea he was on, including the now married Katharine Tynan, transformed into Mrs Hinkson. His occult studies and practices continued, now centred on the Golden Dawn. In 1893 he was admitted to its inner circle. He was already a full member of the Second Order (RR et AC) the initials standing for Rosa Rubeae et Aureae Crucis (Rose of Ruby and the Golden Cross) and had received a secret name, DEDI – an acronym of Demon est Deus Inversus (The Devil is God's Opposite). The next step in his initiation involved the ritual of the Path of the Portal. Yeats lay down in a symbolic tomb, 'died' and was reborn, his spirit renewed in the image of Christ. At this time he was as regular and assiduous in practising his invocations of occult spirits as any orthodox Christian or Muslim might be in their own devotions. Staying with

George Pollexfen when his uncle was ill with blood-poisoning, Yeats made use of Kabbalistic symbols and names to repel the demons causing the trouble; his uncle felt a rushing river sweep them away.

Some of his biographers have seen Yeats as a calculating manager of his own career, using his friends and contacts to obtain work, making his way steadily towards his goals of social and literary recognition, and financial independence. But if Yeats had died in 1890, the previous decade, which saw him established as a poet, would have looked like a time of floundering and disjointed activity, much of it prompted by accident. It was by accident that he had met MacGregor Mathers. It was another accident that brought about his first real play. (It is only fair to point out here that Yeats himself did not believe in accidents.)

His very first efforts in creative writing had been in dramatic form. Now he heard much about the theatre from a Chiswick friend, Florence Farr, at that time still in the throes of a long and passionate liaison with George Bernard Shaw. She was a member of the Golden Dawn Order, an actress, and was also involved with selection (in effect dramaturg) for the Avenue Theatre in the West End of London. In 1894, at her request, he wrote a one-act play, 'The Land of Heart's Desire'. It was normal at the time for a 'curtain-raiser' to be shown before the main play of the evening, and this one, first performed at the Avenue Theatre in London in April 1894, was a great success. As with everything he was writing, the thought of Maud lay knitted into the soul of the text, which tells how a 'Faery Child' entices away an impetuous young bride from her bewildered husband. It portrays the elusiveness and untouchability which Maud had for him. The backer of the Avenue's season was Annie Horniman, another in the interlinked constellation of women who were to move around, and in and out of, W.B. Yeats's life. She too was an initiate of the Golden Dawn.

In February 1894 he made his first trip abroad, to visit Mathers and his wife, who had removed to Paris, a city which was the centre of other-worldly cults, where writers such as J.K. Huysmans were flaunting esoteric lore in scandalous novels, and where Villiers de l'Ile–Adam had written 'Le Chateau d'Axel', a drama full of Rosicrucian themes, whose world-renouncing, magic-performing hero and heroine made a profound impression on Yeats, among many others. It was of course also the other point of Maud Gonne's existence: the one that was closed and shadowy to Yeats.

Maud could not see him much. She was ill: in fact two months pregnant with her second child. Millevoye was again the father; they had had intercourse in the crypt of their dead infant son in order to obtain his soul in the child-to-be. Yeats left Paris as unaware of her other life as when he arrived. But his French stay made a deep impression on him; in the intellectual, artistic and spiritual ferment of Paris, very different to Dublin and London, he saw how much his own ideas were also the ideas of the age. Desperately hindered as he was by his minimal knowledge of French – he was a poor linguist – he struggled to absorb what was going on. The bilingual Maud, and Mathers' French wife, both helped him. He had come with letters of introduction to poets like Mallarmé (who ironically was in England), and Verlaine. He discussed writers like Maeterlinck, the arch-symbolist. With Maud he went to see 'Le Chateau d'Axel' performed, and took the text home for further study. In a review of the play he wrote of its two protagonists:

'They are merely metaphors in that divine argument which is carried on from age to age, and perhaps from world to world, about the ultimate truths of existence.'

The visit was a fruitful one, except that his yearning love for Maud remained unrequited. She had treated him as a good friend, and one with common interests; but there was no hint of reciprocatory passion, no glimmer of the one-time brother-sister dream. He returned to London with that aching void still unfilled in his heart.

A heightened poetic confidence as well as greater financial resources helped to make the Paris trip a success. In London, during 1891, Yeats had been a co-founder of the Rhymers' Club, an association of poets who met weekly in the Cheshire Cheese Tavern, off Fleet Street, to read their work, discuss the art and techniques of poetry, and indulge in literary gossip. Although many different interests overlapped among the members, who included Aubrey Beardsley, Arthur Symons, Lionel John-

son, Ernest Rhys and the Scottish poet John Davidson,
the centre of interest was neither Ireland nor the psychic
world, but poetry. The Rhymers' Club helped to establish Yeats not simply as an Irish poet – which at the time
might also have carried the connotation of 'provincial',
but as a poet of the English language. His attitude to
the use of English had become a point of difference
between Yeats and such nationalists as Douglas Hyde,
who believed that the regeneration of Ireland required
the regeneration and full use of its ancient Gaelic language. Yeats was firmly of the view that English was an
international language owned by its users and that it
could fully convey the aspirations of Irish writers and
thinkers. The Rhymers' Club was very much identified
with the *fin de siècle* decadence associated with the *Savoy*
and *Yellow Book* magazines, and Yeats's poetic evolution
was carrying him far past this fashionable attitude. He
could sense his divergence, writing in 1892:

'I well remember the irritated silence that fell upon a
noted gathering of the younger English imaginative
writers once, when I tried to explain a philosophy
of poetry in which I was profoundly interested, and
tried to show the dependence, as I conceived it, of all
great art and literature upon conviction and heroic life.'

To his fellow-rhymers, he felt, literature was not the
handmaid of humanity but 'had become instead a terrible queen'.

CHAPTER FOUR

*C*ELTIC MYSTERIES

Yeats was spreading his wings. Much of 1894 he spent
with Uncle George in Sligo, writing poems and also revis-
ing those already published: a pattern that was to become
familiar. He had new friends in the area, the aristocratic
Gore-Booth family in their big house, Lissadell. He had
met Constance Gore-Booth in London, where she was
an art student, and felt drawn to her and even more to her
sister Eva. Like Maud, they were to show themselves as
unconventional members of a conventional Ascendancy
family. He was to delineate their youth in marvellous lines:

> The light of evening, Lissadell,
> Great windows open to the south,
> Two girls in silk kimonos, both
> Beautiful, one a gazelle.
> ('In Memory of Eva Gore-Booth and
> Con Markiewicz', *1927)*

– and was very conscious of the social 'breakthrough'
that had been achieved; despite their common adherence
to the Church of Ireland, there had been no social contact
between the Gore-Booths and the merchants of Sligo. His
younger brother Jack got married in that same year. In
1895 Yeats celebrated his thirtieth birthday. In a sense his

adolescence had lasted long into his twenties, protracted by financial dependence and the overwhelming presence of his father. During 1895 he had an experience which was to be influential and remain with him for the rest of his life. From a stay in Sligo he had gone to visit Douglas Hyde at Roscommon, and together they had been rowed up Lough Key to Castle Rock, an empty castle on a little island. There was a stone platform where

> 'meditative persons might pace to and fro. I planned a mystical Order which should buy or hire the castle, and keep it as a place where its members might retire for a while for contemplation, and where we might establish mysteries like those of Eleusis or Samothrace; and for ten years to come my most impassioned thought was a vain attempt to find philosophy and to create ritual for that Order.'

So wrote Yeats in *Autobiographies*. That year he published *Poems*, in which he gave revised versions of numerous early poems with whose diction or rhythms he was no longer satisfied. He also joined a breakaway London element of the Irish Republican Brotherhood. This was the Irish National Alliance, another secret organization, headed by Dr Mark Ryan. At the end of 1895 he moved out of the family home to share lodgings with his friend Arthur Symons, the poet and critic who shared his interest in French culture. His sister Lollie fully expected his return, but it was not to happen. For the first time since his meeting with Maud, he also formed a romantic friendship

with a woman. Maud was far from forgotten, but he
had made himself accept that she was unattainable. This
lady made no bones about her attainability; she had
been impressed by 'The Land of Heart's Desire' and was
powerfully attracted to the tall, intense poet with his
expressive gestures and his Irish accent.

Like a flock of rooks circling in changing patterns
round a solitary tower, two inter-related groups of wom-
en were to play vital parts in Yeats's emotional life. This
lady, Olivia Shakespear, his first mistress, had a daughter, Dorothy, who married Ezra Pound, who had been
Yeats's literary secretary; Dorothy was the best friend
of Georgie Hyde-Lees, whom Yeats was to marry. The
brooding presence of Maud Gonne in his life was to be
complemented by her daughter Iseult.

Olivia was married to a wealthy solicitor in a love-
less match, but in practice was leading an independent
life in the literary circles that she enjoyed. In many
ways she was a more cultured person than Yeats, who
still felt himself to be provincial and hampered by his
lack of education. Their approach to physical love was
a very gradual one, hampered by Yeats's reserve, lack of
money and Olivia's desire not to compromise her social
position. When he was in Ireland they wrote to each
other; in London they met in parks or travelled on suburban trains. Even to his friend Symons, Yeats referred to
Olivia as 'Diana Vernon', to keep her identity secret. At
last, early in 1896, Yeats rented himself rooms in Woburn
Buildings (now 5 Woburn Walk) in the Bloomsbury

district and close to the British Museum. Here, with
due precautions, Olivia could visit him in private, and
they became lovers. With uncanny precision of timing,
Maud Gonne wrote to him at this time to tell him that
he had appeared to her in a room in Dublin as she sat
with friends. Nevertheless, the tentative steps with Olivia went on. Like a young married couple they went
to buy cheap furniture, including, to Yeats's embarrass-
ment, a large double bed. Their happy relationship lasted
almost to the end of the year. Whether she knew or not
what was going on, Maud Gonne began to write Yeats
letters that almost held out affection. That summer he
travelled in the west of Ireland with his friend Symons
(Olivia was in Italy with her husband). Maud wrote
that she wished she could have joined him. In another
letter she added: 'I shall hope to see you in Paris in the
winter.' Such slight, perhaps unintentional, tugs on the
leash were enough to cool Yeats's ardour in the affair
with Olivia. She could not fail to notice it, and one day
left his rooms in tears. With the callous objectivity of an
artist, Yeats preserved the moment in verses for Maud:

> '. . . I had a beautiful friend
> And dreamed that the old despair
> Would end in love in the end:
> She looked in my heart one day
> And saw your image was there;
> She has gone weeping away.'
> ('The Lover Mourns for the Loss of Love', 1898)

The 1896 visit to Ireland also resulted in the most important friendship of his life, other than that with Maud. Yeats and Symons had been staying with the Catholic aesthete Edward Martyn at Tillyra Castle in Galway before and after their visit to the Aran Islands. Yeats outraged Martyn by practising his Kabbalistic chants in an empty room which happened to be above the chapel where Martyn performed his own more conventional devotions. The visions seen by Yeats following these exercises included a centaur and a naked woman shooting arrows at a star (an image that recurs in his late poem 'Parnell's Funeral'). Despite this, when Symons returned to London, Yeats stayed on. A country neighbour, Lady Gregory, came to call. They had met before in London, but here in Ireland, her conversation with him rapidly kindled a keen interest in the man, his works and his plans for such things as a Celtic theatre. He was invited to her house at Coole, not far away. Augusta Gregory was the widow of a British colonial administrator, Sir William Gregory; a man thirty-five years older than her, and had a teenage son, Robert. She had had an affair with the poet Wilfred Scawen Blunt. With William Yeats, thirteen years her junior, she would be far more of a surrogate mother than anything else. She was soon a confidante of his passions and personal dreams as well as of his plans.

Lady Gregory, with her grand house, her domestics, her well-stocked wine cellar, her money, her common sense and efficiency, and her enthusiasm for literature, was indeed in all respects the mother Yeats might have

craved. Her age, her short stature and plump figure all
contributed to the attributes of a mother-figure for
him, compared with the tall goddess who still possessed
his sexual fantasies. Lady Gregory herself had written
poems about her love-affair with Blunt. As Yeats left, he
was invited to return in the following year, and in fact he
returned to Coole regularly for twenty summers. And
another correspondent was added to Yeats's ever-growing
address book.

In December 1896 Yeats took up Maud Gonne's sug-
gestion and returned to Paris. He rented a room and
stayed for several weeks. As with the first visit, it provided
him with great mental stimulation, though no progress
in his courtship of Maud (who must have gone to some
trouble to keep the infant Iseult out of the way). They
spent much time together, but the conversation was kept
to Irish matters, political and cultural. She joined with
him in his efforts to set out the basis of the Celtic Order
of Mysteries, deriving from his Lough Key vision, though
he also spent a lot of time with MacGregor Mathers,
an expert on ritual and himself a Celt in spirit; he had
assumed a Scottish title as 'Comte de Glenstrae'. Yeats
had drifted away from the political arena; Maud was
very much an *engagée*, making speeches on behalf of
Irish nationalism, agitating both publicly and privately
for this and related causes, and prominent on the British government's list of subversive persons. The national
movement itself, still unrecovered from the fall and death
of Parnell, was full of factionalism. At that time it was

chiefly concerned with arguing over the celebration of
the hundredth anniversary of the death of Wolfe Tone
in 1898. The combative Maud inevitably was embroiled
in the internecine strife, and it was to give her support
that Yeats, somewhat wearily and wearyingly, again took
an active part on his return to London.

It has often been pointed out how Yeats leaned on others in the development and progress of his career. But
he was not exclusively a taker. In Paris at this time he
also met John Millington Synge, a fellow-countryman
then studying French at the University and with ambitions to be a literary critic. Pleased to find a congenial
young Irishman, Yeats energetically dissuaded him from
criticism and, still himself glowing with recollections of
Aran, the Irish peasantry and the Irish West, persuaded
Synge that his future lay as an Irish writer. Perhaps Synge
would have taken that path anyway, but Yeats may claim
the credit for pointing him in the direction which led to
'The Playboy of the Western World' and 'Deirdre of the
Sorrows'. Again Paris reminded him of the European
dimension of thought, both through the still very active
psychic and occult groups which he frequented, where
drugs were much in vogue to enhance perception; and
through literature. Absurd, ironic and satirical new plays
like Alfred Jarry's 'Ubu Roi', which provided a vivid
counterpoint to his earlier viewing of 'Axel', showed him
how quickly the tide of literary innovation was moving; and, in a man already familiar with the concept of
renewal, helped awaken the idea that self-renewal was as

important in the business of being a writer as it was in the search for the keys to the world of spirit.

On June 22nd, 1897, he and Maud were both in the National Club in Dublin when, as anticipated, there were nationalist riots against the celebration that day of Queen Victoria's Jubilee. As the police charged into the rioters, Maud wanted to go out into the mêlée; Yeats had the doors locked, for her own safety, and to her fury. It was not only their political agendas that were different, with hers more extreme in every way, but their level of personal commitment. To Maud Gonne, a heroic death on the barricades was a worthy ending. Yeats had no instinct towards martyrdom. The politics of Irish nationalism had become Maud's life-work. His life-work, grounded far more deeply in Ireland, was his writing. His plays, poems and stories might help the cause but their creation was not driven by a political will. Although his desire for her lost none of its intensity, they were now clearly treading different paths. Politics no longer united them, and Maud, though she cultivated her clairvoyance and never lost interest in the occult, had forsaken the Golden Dawn, not caring for its highly organized hieratic and very male-dominated structure.

Yeats went on to his second stay at Coole. He and Lady Gregory had embarked on an exploration of Irish folklore and the oral tradition. The country farms and hamlets of the district proved to be rich sources of stories. They discussed their dream of a national Irish theatre with visitors to Coole, including AE and Edward

Martyn. Yeats returned to London refreshed, and even there Lady Gregory's kindness pursued him, with food parcels, gifts of furnishings and money.

Her reward was his friendship, a growing degree of admission to his inner confidences – Yeats was not in any case a reticent person – the sharing of a congenial task in their folklore research, and the sense of sharing in a great project with the theatre plan. In return she gave her hospitality, her respect for his genius, financial support – an invaluable cushion of moral support.

An increasing degree of comfort in his life did not stop him from working hard. At this time he was very much concerned with writing prose in the form of short stories that explored some of his most basic themes. In these stories, some of them collected as *The Secret Rose* (1897), he evolved characters who would also recur often in his poems: Michael Robartes, the rough magician, spiritual and sensual at the same time, dedicated to exploring the depths of pagan mysticism; Owen Aherne, the heretical Catholic for whom Catholicism is an incomplete answer; and Red Hanrahan, the countryman, teacher and visionary poet steeped in the folk tradition. Hanrahan is closer to the earth than the mystic heavens, a man alive to the seasons and the basic physical activities of country life, its cycle of seed, growth, harvest and winter expressed in human, animal and vegetable existence, and always ready to tumble a wench at the back of a hedge. These figures seem to be almost avatars of Yeats himself, the first two expressing different directions of his thought,

and used, like robots in a radioactive chamber, to enter
territory that he himself recognized as obscure or even
dangerous. In some poems he was to call them up as
though they had the same objective reality as as historical figures like Swift, or the same rooting in Irish legend
as Cuchulain. The stories themselves are slow-moving,
using exotic language, full of visions expressed in self-
consciously beautiful prose, and deliberately difficult; as
Yeats wrote to O'Leary, they were: 'an honest attempt
towards that aristocratic esoteric Irish literature, which
has been my chief ambition. We have a literature for the
people but nothing yet for the few.' Yeats was not setting
out to court the market-place.

In March 1898 the much-discussed theatre plans began
to take form, as Yeats struggled with the practicalities of
finding a hall and getting a license, as well as fuelling
the debate about what a national theatre should be. A
wider circle than his own little coterie was interested in
this question, and as with the earlier squabbles over the
publishing of a collection of Irish literature – a battle
which Yeats had lost – there were different views. There
were people who saw no reason why Willie Yeats should
snatch up the project and run away with it, and others
who saw many reasons why he should not. Writing in
the nationalist journal *An Claidheamh Solais* ('The Bright
Sword'), Padraig Pearse dismissed Yeats as an English poet
of the third or fourth rank, and as such harmless. 'But
when he seeks to start an "Irish Literary Theatre", it
is time to crush him'. For the committed nationalists,

Yeats's London home, his English and Ascendancy friends, his indifference to the Irish language, were evidence that he was an obstacle and an enemy. But they also discovered that on his chosen ground, Yeats was a man of action. He had learned from the Literary Club episode, and was ready to flatter, cajole, bully, impress. The poet, whose best-known work was still the escapist idyll of Innisfree, was now an able committee man and a capable organizer. The Wolfe Tone centenary programme, with events in London as well as in Dublin, also claimed much of his time and energy.

The skirmishings and manoeuvrings of all this were as nothing compared to the emotional tumult that awaited him. Maud Gonne and he had been sporadically together much of the time. Earlier in the year she had broken her arm by falling from a wagon which had been her platform to address a street demonstration. She and he talked much about dreams, and every reference she made to her own inner life touched Yeats's quivering passion for her. Maud sent him earth from the prehistoric Newgrange site, and water from the Boyne, so that he might touch his lips, his ears, his eyelids and breast, and dream Celtic dreams. As ever, the faintest hint of interest from her made him hasten to her side. In a meeting late that year, he told her he had dreamed that he had kissed her lips. She recounted a dream in which she and he had been joined in marriage by the Celtic deity Lugh. And, for the first time, they did exchange real kisses. Yeats's hopes must have been at a ten-year high, but the very next day, she dashed them, telling him that she could never be his wife. He learned now about Millevoye, about her children, of that life in France about which he had chosen not to speculate, while writing poems of longing, of tender admiration to his virginal ideal. Maud explained that she was now repelled and afraid of sexual love. Yeats listened in mounting horror and distress.

His dreams had been most rudely trodden on, his finest work he now knew to have been written to a sham. Even though he had no claims upon Maud, he had been a dupe and a fool. In his distress he wrote to Lady Gregory, then in Venice; she returned to Ireland to give him support and advice. She met Maud privately, and formed the view that Maud was damaging to Yeats. Close to physical and mental breakdown, he retreated to his uncle George at Sligo. Encouraged by George Pollexfen, he went to Paris in January 1899. His love for Maud was undiminished. Perhaps it was even greater. The aim of the visit was to propose marriage to her, but she rejected it. He returned to London, sad, far from clear about his own future. Like some triple-distilled liquor, evoked into a clear, dry fineness by a long and difficult process. His love for Maud became a concentrated thing, and he wrote to Lady Gregory to say how it had become bitterer, and harder. But it did not fade.

If there were angels in his life, like Lady Gregory, there were also imps. Yeats, to whom candour was natural, and who, until his old age, had quite a shockable Puritan streak in him, felt some admiration for those writers who, like Emile Zola, wrote naturalistically of 'true life' as they saw, or imagined, it; and for writers of the worldly confessional sort, like Frank Harris. These tendencies combined in George Moore, the Irish novelist whom he had known now for some years, since the time of the *Savoy* magazine. Yeats took himself seriously. Moore, like Ezra Pound later, had an urge to debunk what he saw as excessive solemnity or portentousness. Also, he relished mischief-making for its own sake. The friendship of the two men would wax and wane, and often seem more like an ongoing verbal duel. Moore's first interference with Yeats's schemes came with the rehearsals for the opening season of the Irish Literary Theatre. For this, Yeats had recruited his erstwhile patron, Florence Farr, to set up a company of actors, rehearse in London, and bring the plays to Dublin for performance. There were two, his own 'The Countess Kathleen', and Edward Martyn's 'The Heather Field'. Moore, whom Lady Gregory had brought in as a director of the Literary Theatre, disrupted the rehearsal of his cousin Martyn's play and almost caused a fight. Then rumours were spread that Yeats's play offended against Catholic orthodoxy, which might have worried Yeats less if Martyn, the main financial backer of the project, had not been an extremely devout Catholic himself. It was also regarded by the more idealistic nationalists as an attack on the Irish people. Yeats went to the trouble of getting police to guard the theatre on the opening night. But the evening, and the first short season of the Irish Literary Theatre, were both peaceful and successful.

Yeats and Moore began collaboration on a play based on the classic Celtic love story of Diarmid and Grainne. He was also still working on the long-gestating verse play 'The Shadowy Waters', a symbolist drama in Celtic garb, influenced by works such as 'Axel's Castle' and the plays of Maeterlinck. In that year (1899) Yeats's friend Arthur Symons published his study *The Symbolist Movement in Literature*, with which Yeats had helped him and which was dedicated to Yeats. It was apt that Yeats published *The Wind Among the Reeds,* in the same year, a collection of poems, some of which went back as far as 1892. The progress of the poet, the fruits of his obedience to his own maxim, 'hammer your thoughts into unity' can be seen in the contrast between the earlier and the later poems in this volume. 'The Song of the Old Mother', from 1894, is an entirely competent short poem that might have been written by any number of contemporary poets, George Meredith, for example. But most of the poems are unmistakably Yeats. Richard Ellmann, in his biography of Yeats, recognized the mesmeric quality of Yeats's verse, and points out how in 'The Lover Bids His Beloved Be at Peace' (written for Olivia, 1895) 'No word has any explicit meaning; we neither know nor feel compelled to ask what are the Shadowy Horses of Disaster. . .' But the lushness of the text is undeniably cloying. 'The Song of Wandering Aengus', written only two years later, could not have come, in its fusion of yearning thought, perfectly chosen words, irregular yet utterly appropriate rhyme-scheme, and musicality of rhythm, from any hand but Yeats's, but its triumph is its understated spareness and directness of tone:

> 'Though I am old with wandering
> Through hollow lands and hilly lands,
> I will find out where she has gone,
> And kiss her lips and take her hands;
> And walk among long dappled grass,
> And pluck till time and times are done
> The silver apples of the moon,
> The golden apples of the sun.'

The precision with which Yeats delineates his images, and the ease with which his finest lyrics may be read aloud, belies the effort that went into their creation. Few of his poems, and none of the major ones, were not drafted and redrafted, revised and re-revised, until he felt they conveyed what he wanted to convey. What he wanted to express was very often not a statement, or thought, or a description, but something more elusive, if not less real: a state of mind, a perceived situation, the fluid mingling of two or more images to produce a resonance that might give a moment's heightened insight into the forces controlling life. It was a painstaking business, and Yeats's genius certainly was one which was prepared to take infinite pains. Ellmann shows how one of short lyrics in this collection, 'To His Heart, Bidding It Have No Fear', developed from a thirty-six line first attempt, whose first lines ran:

'Impetuous heart give heed to my rime
The tale of tales may never be told
Cover it up with a lonely tune
Cover it up with a fitful dream
Give help to my heart great journeyman
Who hid away the infinite fold
With the pale stars and the wan moon . . .'

through versions including:

'Impetuous heart, be still, be still,
Your sorrowful love may never be told;
Cover it up with a lonely tune;
He who could bend all things to His will
Has covered the door of the infinite fold
With the pale stars and the wandering moon.'

to the final form:

'Be you still, be you still, trembling heart;
Remember the wisdom out of the old days:
Him who trembles before the flame and the flood,
And the winds that blow through the starry ways,
Let the starry winds and the flame and the flood
Cover over and hide, for he has no part
With the proud, majestical multitude.'

The love poems in *The Wind Among the Reeds* include
those written for Olivia as well as those for Maud; Yeats

arranged them in a non-chronological order in order to prevent them being seen as a sort of autobiographical commentary. To read them was a wry experience for Olivia Shakespear, but she and he had resumed their friendship. No longer his lover, she became one of his most trusted confidantes.

Most of his life was now being spent away from his family. But he was staying with his parents at Chiswick for Christmas 1899. On the 3rd of January 1900, his mother died. Despite her invalid condition it was unexpected, and only Willie and his father were at her deathbed.

He knew that he had never been her favourite child. In their succession of small houses, young Yeats was present for the births of five siblings and the deaths of two. His brother Bobby, who died at three, had been preferred by his mother; the late-coming Jack had always been closer to her, despite having been shipped out to Sligo for most of his childhood. But she was demonstrative to no-one. Her elder daughter, Lily, said 'She asked no sympathy and gave none.' Soon after her marriage, Susan Yeats allowed silence and depression to rule her life. Only in Sligo, and for a time in Howth, did she seem to emerge from herself. When she chose to be articulate, at the time when he was still a young boy, it was usually to complain or be critical. The effect on her eldest son of this withdrawal into herself and the consequent lack of displayed love and affection – perhaps there was ultimately none to show – has been much pondered on by Yeats scholars. He referred little to his mother in his copious autobiographical writings. Her death prevented Jack from painting for several months; Willie was soon off to tea with Lady Gregory at her London apartment, planning the next stage of the Literary Theatre. There was no poem to mark the passing of his mother; her spirit, uncommunicative in life, remained so in death and there is no record that Yeats sought to achieve contact with her on the 'astral plane'. Her contribution to his life was passive; her influence minimal. It may be speculated that his slowness to learn as a child had something to do with her; it has been speculated that his often demonic energy and activity were driven by an effort to win recognition from a silent and critical mother; that his explorations of Irish culture exemplified some kind of way back to a hoped-for mother-embrace; that his lifelong spiritual quest was in response to the emotional deprivation she inflicted. Her main legacy was his continuing worry about his own sanity and the possibility that his life might follow hers into anomie. Several members of the numerous Pollexfen clan had suffered from mental disorder; once his mother's sister Agnes, having liberated herself from some institution, turned up on the Chiswick doorstep and caused much trouble until the vexed Yeatses summoned the attendants from the 'home' to come and take her away.

CHAPTER FIVE

'VISIONS OF TRUTH IN THE DEPTHS OF THE MIND'

Despite the infighting and the difficulties, the success of the first short season of the Literary Theatre, featuring one of his own plays, encouraged Yeats to continue his work both as a dramatic writer and as a theatrical presenter. There was a satisfaction to be had, for a dramatic poet, in seeing his work make its impact on an appreciative audience, that the normal lyric poet, however widely read, would never know. When the plays had an ultimate political purpose, however concealed, this satisfaction had an additional edge of gratification. Yeats could feel that by renewing Irish culture to the new generation of theatre-goers, he was being as useful to the cause as Maud on her makeshift rostrum in the street. Although he was never a committed man of the theatre – it was always there to serve his aims – he was genuinely attracted to it, and particularly by the ways in which theatrical performances could match the intensity and inner drama of ritual. From 1901 the Literary Theatre was able to use the talents of two Dublin brothers, the actors William and Frank Fay, who had evolved a style of acting which reduced movement and focused on speech, which was very much in line with Yeats's own notion of how his plays should be performed (the influence of Irving had clearly been pared down). The Fays, untrained amateurs, were clearly fine actors, but perhaps the lack of others as good, the small halls and their small stages, and the tight budget on which the company had to run, all influenced Yeats's reductive view of theatrical presentation, which eventually led him to welcome and imitate the Japanese Noh theatre, when he discovered its existence.

Performance and self-presentation were essential aspects of his own being. The Hamlet walk and the ostentatious shabbiness had become modified into a persona of studied style. As he became more comfortably off, observers noted the beauty of his clothes, cut well from soft materials. He himself, a tall and imposing figure, with the escaping fore-lock above the big, soulful, benevolent-looking face, with its mild myopic eyes, long upper lip and strong, sensuous mouth (though the same face could wear a forbidding scowl on occasion), was an attractive man with a defi-nite presence. Like other poets of outgoing personality and great inner intensity, Robert Burns for example, his force seemed to charge the air around him. Like Charles Dickens, he was a very successful reciter of his own works in public, and also lectured well, though he never made such an industry of either as Dickens had done or as Oscar Wilde did, for a time. In those pre-radio and TV days, there was a large and avid middle-brow public, in England and in the USA, for cultural talks by more-or-less well-known literary figures.

The collaboration with Moore revealed the difference between the pragmatic writer, keen to make the piece as theatrical as possible, and the man of letters, who did not wish to sacrifice the poetic development of the narrative to the crude demands of theatre for clearly defined scenes, dramatic happenings and climactic moments. Nevertheless the play was completed and successfully performed. After that, Yeats did not seek to write in collaboration, except with people like Lady Gregory (whose writing he encouraged) where he could exert unchallenged control rather than have to argue with the peppery Moore, who saw himself as the senior figure.

Florence Farr was much involved with his dramatic work, and also participated in developing a form of verse recitation accompanied by a lute-like instrument, the psaltery. The style was incantatory, somewhat dreamy, highly suitable to most of the poems he had written so far. There was more than a trace of 'Celtic Twilight' about the approach. The Irish writer St John Ervine, who disliked Florence, wrote in his biography of Shaw:

'This chanting was called "cantilating", and was a melancholy noise. I remember a night when she persuaded W.B.Yeats, into whose affection she passed when G.B.S. had done with her, to lift up his voice in a depressing howl while she plucked her strings to pieces. Yeats, who loathed and detested music, became so pleased with his singing that his friends had difficulty in preventing him from "cantilating"

every time they spent an evening in his dark rooms
in Woburn Buildings, behind the Euston Road.'

Ervine wielded a malicious pen. The chanting was
normally done by Florence. It was true, however, that
Yeats was tone-deaf. He had no ear for music, but his
sense of rhythm and feeling for the nuances of the spoken
word were exceptionally keen.

For a short time, in the mid-1890s, his friendship with
Florence became a passionate one; for the first time since
Olivia Shakespear had left weeping, he was involved in a
sexual relationship, but it was a grand passion to neither
of them, and eventually petered out. Nothing and no-
one could replace Maud. In her own autobiography she
recorded his proposal to her in 1901, when they went
together to look at the Stone of Destiny in Westminster
Abbey (it is now in Edinburgh Castle but to Yeats and
Maud, the Lia Fail was an Irish symbol), part of the
dialogue reads:

'Oh Maud, why don't you marry me and give up
this tragic struggle and live a peaceful life? I could
make such a beautiful life for you among artists and
writers who would understand you.'
'Willie, are you not tired of asking that question?
How often have I told you to thank the gods I will
not marry you. You would not be happy with me.'
'I am not happy without you.'
'Oh yes, you are, because you make beautiful poetry

out of what you call your unhappiness and you are happy in that.'

The style of the 'beautiful poetry' was changing. Yeats was far from insular in his literary interests and awareness. He knew about the work of such disparate writers as the French absurdist Alfred Jarry, the German realist Gerhart Hauptmann and the occult pre-Expressionist Swedish playwright August Strindberg, even if his linguistic limitations prevented him from reading them. His own maturing thought was leading him away from the brilliant but self-regarding 'Rose' poems, whose language, while not 'poetic' in the artificial sense (he always hated such usages as 'ere', only found in verse, was intentionally high-flown and distinguished. The 'populist' style was always available for him to deploy. From the days of his collections of Sligo folk-tales, he had known and appreciated the simplicity of approach and the directness of language used in the stories of the English-speaking country Irish. Such charming poems as 'The Fiddler of Dooney' from 1892 show how well he himself could pluck that string. But up till now, that style had been used only for such incidental or folksy poems, never applied to his central themes.

'On Baile's Strand' and 'Cathleen ni Houlihan' (the latter written with Lady Gregory) show this stylistic move well under way. They incorporate prose as well as verse, and a wider range of characters from the tortured poetic personas, the pale kings and paler queens, who preceded

them. For the part of Grainne in Diarmid and Grania,
Yeats had hoped for Mrs Patrick Campbell, the dominant
actress of the time. For his heroine in 'Cathleen ni Houlihan', he wanted, and got, Maud Gonne. She was not
without experience as an actress, and this role, in which
the apparent old ragged crone throws off her rags to reveal herself as a queenly personification of Ireland, suited
her own melodramatic character. The play was a great
success despite its opening in the completely unsuitable
St Teresa's church hall. This was in April 1902. Yeats and
his beloved could share a sense of achievement, as creator
and interpreter, of a much-praised patriotic drama. But
otherwise she remained at arm's length.

On his summer visit to Coole that year, Yeats met a
wealthy New York lawyer, John Quinn, a second-gen-
eration Irish immigrant, who had become a patron of
art and literature, with a keen interest in the land of his
fathers. Quinn was to become a significant figure not
only to W.B. Yeats but to his father and sisters as well. He
had already been in touch with John Butler Yeats. Although his main contribution was to organize lectures
in the USA and to look after the publication of Yeats's
work in the States at a time when copyright was hard to
enforce, he also opened up a new front in Yeats's intellectual strategy by sending him the English translation
of Friedrich Nietzsche's 'Also Sprach Zarathustra'. Nietzsche's loftiness of utterance, utter lack of sentimentality,
and determination to secure a heroic clarity of vision, all
had immediate appeal to Yeats. Nietzsche had been dead

for two years, and mad for a decade before. His political thoughts, including his contempt for both liberal ethics and democracy, were to find echoes in Yeats's later views and behaviour. His views on the death of God do not appear to have troubled the poet, who was excited by Nietzsche's separation of the soul's movement into Dionysiac and Apollonian phases; applying this to himself, he found that it worked. He was moving into the 'joyful and self-sufficient' Apollonian phase, he wrote to George Russell. He rapidly wrote a Nietzschean drama, 'Where There Is Nothing', with an Irish setting, influenced by his new knowledge of its great country houses and their often far from predictable families. The hero, one of the 'landed gentry', throws off the assumptions and traditions of his social group to pursue his anarchistic ideas to their logical conclusion. He ends his days in a monastery. At this time Robert Gregory, only son of Lady Gregory, was almost twenty-one, a student at Oxford. His views were quite conventional; someone like Constance Gore-Booth would be a more likely model. The play was to have been a further collaboration with George Moore, but Yeats had had enough of that; there was a break and a quarrel.

In 1901 Queen Victoria had died. In the previous year she had made a state visit to Dublin, which her government had hoped would both help to damp down Irish nationalism and encourage Irishmen to join the British Army, then engaged in the Boer War in South Africa. Neither aim was wholly successful. There were protests as well as acclamations. Maud Gonne made a famous, jeering speech. Though Irish soldiers joined up, an Irish Brigade was also formed to fight for the Boers against the British. Its exploits, under Major John McBride, were widely publicized in the nationalist press and at public meetings. McBride's name became famous.

Yeats was one of many to feel that this man, hitherto unknown, should play a large part in Irish political life on his return.

McBride's return was to have a drastic impact on Yeats's own life. In 1901, Maud Gonne had accompanied him on a fund-raising tour of the United States. The hero of the Boer War came to Paris early in 1903, to be fêted by the small Irish nationalist community there. In February 1903 William Yeats received a telegram to let him know that Maud Gonne and John McBride were to be married. It was a terrible blow to Yeats. He had suffered through and risen above the news of the Millevoye liaison, and accepted her claim that physical love now was repellent to her. After ten years, all his ardour remained on offer to her, and now, in no time at all, she had given herself to an adventurer. The cup was a foamingly bitter one. It was a repudiation not only of him as a man, but of the kind of man he had chosen to be. She had gone to the man of action, and spurned the man of thought; embraced the man of extremes and left the man of moderation to mourn. At least before he had been able to console himself that if she was not for him, she was not for any other man; now once again he had to look back on the poems he had written to her, sublime

poems. But for all their carefully wrought beauty, they
had not penetrated past the mask she wore for him. He
was love's fool.

He retreated to the haven of Coole, where a winter
storm had wrought havoc among the trees. The momentum of his external life sustained him, as did the
care of Lady Gregory, who had never been an admirer
of Maud's. Eventually he would make poetry out of
the wound she had dealt him, but it took him several
years. In December 1908 he wrote, in 'No Second Troy':

> 'Why should I blame her, that she fill my days
> With misery . . .
> What could have made her peaceful with a mind
> That nobleness made simple as a fire,
> With beauty like a tightened bow, a kind
> That is not natural in an age like this,
> Being high and solitary and most stern?'

She was an element, she was archaic, of a unique sort –
he forged splendid phrases to create for himself and the
world a satisfactory image of her who would not give
herself to his yearning heart or to his physical embrace –

> 'Why, what could she have done, being what she is?
> Was there another Troy for to burn?'

Yeats was now a significant figure in the literary world,
his status perhaps more secure in London than in Dublin,

where Padraig Pearse, J.F. Taylor, and Frank Hugh
O'Donnell and his friends were hostile. In his London
rooms he was 'at home' on Monday evenings to his
friends and admirers. Around his table, as they consumed
the homely nourishing fare cooked up by his cockney
landlady, Mrs Old, they talked about literature, politics
and literary folk. It was not a brilliant era for English
poetry – of its great late-nineteenth-century figures,
Swinburne remained alive but his great work was far
behind him (when he died in 1909 Yeats was to say: 'Now
I am king of the cats'). Hardy, in remote Dorset, was still
little-appreciated as a poet. Yeats, with his commanding
presence, and a substantial body of published work, was
the leading poet of the London literary scene. And, in its
absorptive way, the English establishment sought to draw
him into it. Yeats's affability helped. He was an entertaining as well as an eminent dinner guest. Good food and
good wine were certainly among his pleasures. Other
Irish writers, like George Moore, also mingled in the
English social scene, but they did not have the nationalist connections that Yeats had. Some of his friends, not
least Maud, who had come to loathe everything that
England stood for, saw his hob-nobbing with English
politicians and the English aristocracy as evidence of his
insincerity, or even of treachery. Yeats was to become
friendly with men like H.H. Asquith, Prime Minister
from April 1908, and Winston Churchill, both of them
men of the Empire who regarded Ireland as a trouble-
some and irritating sideshow that diverted too much of

Britain's political energy. In 1910, not without some doubts, he would accept a civil list pension as a tribute to his poetic achievements. This caused some derision in Dublin, but Yeats felt he had earned it. He had a London identity; his home was there – with the years at Godolphin, the evenings at William Morris's, the long days in the British Museum, London, as well as Sligo and Dublin, had contributed to the shaping of him.

In 1905 he celebrated his fortieth birthday. The hero-poets of his youth, Keats, Shelley, Byron, had all been dead before they reached that age – thirty-six was the age at which genius died, or so it was said. Perhaps that was what James Joyce had in mind, on his first meeting with Yeats in Dublin. Yeats was thirty-nine; his twenty-two-year-old visitor, as arrogant as the young Yeats himself had been, and a good deal more cocksure, said: 'I cannot be of help to you; you are too old.' Yeats took the impudence in good part; he admired Joyce's work then and later, even when it mocked at him and his own poems. His own genius was far from spent. Much in his life took him away from writing at this time, however. A protracted American lecture tour in late 1903, the affairs of the theatre company, and turmoil in the Hermetic Order of the Golden Dawn all made heavy demands on him.

Since 1897, the rapport between Yeats and MacGregor Mathers had been wearing steadily thinner. In that year Yeats and other London members had struggled against Mathers' desire to expel Annie Horniman from the Order. Miss Annie Horniman, the wealthy heiress of a tea importer, played a significant part in Yeats's life, but without emotional engagement on his side. An earnest enquirer into the occult, she had been one of the first members of the Golden Dawn order in England, and her money helped to establish and sustain it. She had also supported MacGregor Mathers, but, since his departure to Paris in 1892, and his increasing involvement with the very masculine world of Freemasonry, she had become somewhat disenchanted and stopped his pension. MacGregor Mathers, from his base in Paris, promptly expelled her from the Order for 'insubordination'. Miss Horniman was eventually reinstated, but further trouble came in 1900, when Mathers asked the London branch to initiate his young protégé Aleister Crowley.

Yeats, who could be gullible enough at times, perceived Crowley to be, as indeed he was, a posturer, a crook, and an unscrupulous dabbler in black magic. The London branch refused Mathers' request, arousing his rage and revealing the proprietorial spirt with which he viewed the organization. He ordered Crowley to take control of the rooms rented by the Order; when the London members resisted by guarding the rooms, he took legal action against them, as well as letting them know he was making war on them by occult means.

Largely due to Yeats's efforts, order was restored, but fresh acrimony soon developed between Florence Farr and Annie Horniman. While for some members the episode caused high excitement, for Yeats it meant spiritual wear and tear that he regretted having to incur. For him the Order was not an end in itself but a means towards spiritual exploration. In an essay of September 1901, published in the *Monthly Review,* he wrote that he believed:

'. . . in what I must call the evocation of spirits though I do not know what they are, in the power of creating magical illusions, in the visions of truth in the depths of the mind when the eyes are closed . . .'

– and he enumerated three basic doctrines as the foundations of magical practice:

'1. That the borders of our mind are ever shifting, and that many minds can flow into one another, as it were, and create or reveal a single mind, a single energy.
2. That the borders of our memories are as shifting, and that our memories are a part of one great memory, the memory of Nature herself.
3. That this great mind and memory can be evoked by symbols.'

This furnishes a useful skeleton key to the extremely complex cabinet of knowledge, beliefs, prejudices, curiosities, semi-conscious and unconscious processes that was Yeats's mind. His concept of the 'Anima Mundi', or world-soul, that resounds in such poems as 'The Second

Coming', and his sense of the ultimate oneness of things:

> 'O chestnut tree, great-rooted blossomer,
> Are you the leaf, the blossom or the bole?
> O body swayed to music, O brightening glance,
> How can we know the dancer from the dance?'
> ('Among School Children')

– are clearly seen here to emerge from his magical studies. At the same time, in Austria, Germany and Switzerland, the fathers of psychoanalysis were working to establish a scientific basis for the unknown workings of the human mind. Yeats read Freud and Jung with interest, and there is a surface resemblance of the Anima Mundi to Jung's concept of the Collective Subconscious, but he was not convinced by mind-science. He often consulted doctors, but he never appears to have considered psychoanalysis.

His support for, and friendship with, Miss Horniman was fruitful in that other driving interest of Yeats in the 1900s – the establishment of a permanent national theatre. A National Theatre Society, with himself as president, was set up. In effect it was a federation of various interested parties, one of which was led by Arthur Griffith and Maud Gonne (whom Griffith greatly admired) and which believed that the theatre had an overtly propagandistic role to play in the nationalist cause. Miss Horniman, after due consultation of the stars and the tarot pack, was ready to put up the money to establish a building for it. The will was there, the funds were there – and so were the plays. Apart from Yeats himself, Edward Martyn, Lady Gregory, AE, and Padraic Colum, who were all writing designedly 'Irish' plays, there was Yeats's young friend from Paris, John M. Synge. He had followed the older poet's advice to follow a literary career, and to visit the Aran Islands. In 1903 he was back in Dublin, with a play, 'Riders to the Sea'. That same year he showed Yeats another, 'In The Shadow of the Glen'.

In November 1903 Yeats crossed the Atlantic to make his first visit to America, and the first of a number of lecture tours there which, organized by John Quinn, gave him useful extra income. As he remarked of himself, his habits were not economical. Despite fees for articles and royalties from poems, his income was small. Lady Gregory gave him frequent subventions, telling him that they were not loans, but could be repaid one day when he could afford to do so. Only this enabled him to preserve his career as a poet, without having to divert attention, time and energy to a salaried job of some unimaginable sort. On his return from America he was made cross by requests for financial help from his sisters, and complained to Lady Gregory of having family responsibilities thrust on him.

Throughout 1904 the work to get a professional theatre company established went on. Yeats and Miss Horniman found a building on the North Bank of the Liffey, the one-time Mechanics' Institute, purchased a lease and or-

ganized building and decorative work. She furnished the
very large sum of £5,000 to underwrite the venture. At
this time she was hoping that Yeats would marry her, but
had to satisfied by acting as his voluntary secretary. Miss
Horniman and Lady Gregory, both benefactors to
the poet, became opponents and Yeats had to exercise
much diplomacy, as in the Golden Dawn, to preserve
peace. The Abbey Theatre opened its doors on December
28th, 1904, with an evening of four short plays. One
was a comedy by Lady Gregory, 'Spreading the News',
two were by Yeats, a revived production of 'Cathleen ni
Houlihan' and the new 'On Baile's Strand'; the fourth
was 'In The Shadow of the Glen'.

His backing of Synge's play had already cost him the
departures from his Theatre Board of Douglas Hyde
and Maud Gonne, both of whom deplored the way in
which Synge portrayed Irish women; a criticism taken
up by others after the first production. The Abbey was
embattled from its start. Yeats was himself a shrewd
publicist who knew the value of controversy for whip-
ping up public interest, and he defended his playwright
with vigour. He was more irritated by the wrangling
and slowness to proceed of the theatre's management
board. By late 1905, this had been reduced to himself,
Lady Gregory and J. M. Synge. Yeats was not an easy-
going president. He was often bad-tempered, angry,
critical. 'My curse on plays That have to be set up in fifty
ways, On the day's war with knave and dolt' he wrote
in 1909 (in 'The Fascination of What's Difficult'). He

was conscious of piloting the theatre through dangerous waters, threatened variously by the Gaelic nationalists, the Church and the British state, which then and for many years later, practised an active censorship of plays. The Abbey was a huge venture in which he had committed his own prestige and his friend's money, and for which he had great hopes. He was not going to allow the indifference of others, or the different wishes of others, to stand in the way. His first Dublin theatre endeavour had been the Irish Literary Theatre, and Literature was still the key-word. The Abbey stood for Art, and for what was modern in stage design as well as in writing. Yeats, who had admired the revolutionary sets of the young Edward Gordon Craig in avant-garde London productions, commissioned him for the Abbey. Dubliners were to be given the most up-to-the-minute theatrical experiences in Europe, whether they wanted to have them or not.

Another group of writers and actors started up a rival concern in May 1906, the Theatre of Ireland. Composed largely of former Abbey associates, including AE, with whom his relations were at this time under heavy strain, and with a much more consciously nationalistic mission, it threatened for a time to be a serious rival. It was the driving energy of Yeats that ensured the survival of the Abbey. A critic whom he had to placate rather than out-argue was his 'angel', Annie Horniman, who had expected to see a wide range of productions and was unhappy with Yeats's policy of putting on Irish plays only. The demonic energy that Yeats put into the early

years of the Abbey made it a profitable concern as well
as an artistically successful one. His own play on a great
Celtic tale of tragic love, 'Deirdre', with Mrs Patrick
Campbell in the title role, was highly successful. But
controversy was never far away, and reached a height
on January 26 1907, the first night of Synge's play 'The
Playboy of the Western World'. Many members of the
audience had come prepared to be outraged, and a
riot developed during the third act. Once again, 'Irish
womanhood' had been insulted. Yeats was lecturing in
Scotland and returned in haste to Dublin. He did not
yield an inch to the pressures. This was far from being a
factitious dispute whipped up gain publicity. He knew
there were formidable forces ranged against him – not
only the offended idealism of some nationalists, or the
begrudgement of professional rivals, but the deep conservatism of the Church, and the strong Jansenist-Puritan
strain of Irish Catholicism. He announced that the play
would continue and demanded that it should be judged
on its merits and not on the prejudices of a *claque*. When
disturbances began on the third night, he had the police
brought in, some people were arrested, and brought to
trial. The play went on. Yeats also staged a public debate
on the whole issue. He saw the matter very clearly, as
freedom of the theatre on the one hand, and its enslave-
ment by the mob on the other. Facing a packed, noisy
and sometimes physically threatening audience, he stated
his views on artistic freedom. He also reminded them
of who he was. The man who had written that intense

patriotic drama 'Cathleen ni Houlihan' was not in business to put on anti-Irish plays. John Butler Yeats came to speak for his son. Together they faced a storm of booing and insult. But the play went on.

Public and private events were exhausting Yeats's energies. Maud Gonne's marriage did not remove her from his thoughts or his preoccupations. In a very short time the union of the heroine and hero proved to be a disaster. Less than three months after their wedding, and pregnant with his child, she knew she had made a disastrous mistake. Early in 1905 she resolved to apply for a judicial separation. She was frank with Yeats, writing:

'Of a hero I had made, nothing remains and the disillusion has been cruel. I am fighting an uneven battle because I am fighting a man without honour or scruples who is sheltering himself and his vices behind the National cause.'

McBride's vices included heavy drinking and a predatory sexual streak that did not shrink from attacking Maud's child Iseult. As with many men of action, his limited intelligence, inability to cope with celebrity status, and social conservatism, made it difficult for him to lead a normal life. He was jealous of Maud's independence and suspected her relationships with other men, including Yeats. Thoughts of his prestige, or her money, made him contest the separation, and many Nationalists supported him. Maud Gonne found that despite a lifetime's work for the cause of Irish nationalism, she could still be typecast as the colonel's daughter – an outsider, an interloper, a woman who did not know her place. Going to the Abbey with Yeats in October 1906, the heroine of the Fenian cause was hissed. She did not give ground. She had adopted Catholicism for McBride's sake and was to remain a pious member of the faith she had embraced. Yeats was sympathetic, unreproachful. She was grateful, and the friendship endured; although their political standpoints were by now quite separate, McBride's continuing role within Sinn Fein made it impossible for Maud to play much part in politics for the next ten years. She spent most of her time in France, in Paris and Normandy, where she had a house on the coast at Colleville, 'Les Mouettes' (shades of the Howth seagulls).

A tour of Italy with Lady Gregory and her son Robert offered Yeats some respite from the cockpit Dublin had become in the summer of 1907. Apart from his visits to Paris, he had not gone further into Europe. Now he saw, in a succession of short stays in a string of beautiful cities, works of art that captivated and enriched his creative imagination for years to come. Florence, Urbino and Ferrara opened his eyes to the extraordinary revelation that the early Renaissance had brought to Europe. Ravenna and Milan touched him even more deeply.

Michelangelo, Mantegna, Bramante and the other Renaissance artists whom he revered had all possessed a strong sense of spirituality. Their humanism, the sense of mathematical form, their delight in metaphysical riddles and puzzles that churches like San Miniato del Monte in Florence showed, all strongly appealed to Yeats. He saw a world of coherence and harmony, based on a union of spiritual and humane values. But in the more ancient churches and mausoleums of Ravenna he felt an even more intense sensation. Their Byzantine mosaics, with their colours unfaded through the centuries, and their glittering, hieratic figures, gave him a powerful sense of mystic connection with that remote era. He was to say that Byzantium in the reign of Justinian, in the sixth century, was the place and the time when he would ideally have wanted to live.

CHAPTER SIX

'I HAVE COME INTO MY STRENGTH AND WORDS OBEY MY CALL'

Though the Yeats family was no longer concentrated in the narrow confines of a suburban house, they remained very much in contact. Willie had moved far beyond his father's tutelage, but John Butler Yeats came to his son's defence in the Abbey's first days of crisis. Lily and Lolly had removed from London to Dublin in 1902. They lived together in a house called Gurteen Dhas, in Dundrum, and worked with a friend, Evelyn Gleeson, in an entirely female-run handicrafts business from a house known as Dun Emer. Lily's skills were in textiles and embroidery, while Lolly had trained as a Froebel teacher and was also an artist. She taught herself the craft of handprinting; and in 1908 the two sisters formed their own business, the Cuala Press. Their elder brother became editorial director of this press, and, although he had made his own publishing arrangements with Macmillan in London, these did not preclude Cuala producing limited first editions of his works (now collectors' pieces). Jack was commissioned to provide illustrations for Cuala Press

books. Relations among the grown-up Yeats children
were not always harmonious, harking back to the kind of
tensions that framed their childhood – Willie and Lolly
were especially liable to fight: their father intervened as
peacemaker when Willie resigned as editorial consultant
to Dun Emer, Lolly having had the temerity to take on
a book by George Russell without asking his advice in
the matter. But their tastes and predilections were very
similar. None of J.B.Yeats's children shared his rational-
ism. They were all capable of seeing fairies when the
light was right.

In the mid years of the decade 1901-10, Yeats had a
more satisfactory love life. Olivia Shakespear had again
become a partner, in a relationship more knowledgeable,
less fraught than the first one. The forty-plus poet also
began to experience the spoils of greatness, in a liaison
with a young London-based Irishwoman – London was
the locale of his sexual life – who had come to his lectures. The affair with Mabel Dickinson was to last until
1913. Placid and amiable, and kept firmly in its own
compartment of his life, it afforded him much comfort,
but was to end in a storm. In December 1908, during a
visit to Paris, he and the still somewhat chastened Maud
had a rapprochement in which he may, as some rather
circumspectly worded correspondence between the two
suggests, have been granted the long yearned-for physical
union which had always been denied him before. If so, it
was not so soul-stirring an experience as to drive him to
celebrate it in verse. Nor was it to lead anywhere. After

his visit, Maud wrote to him in warm and affectionate
words, but making clear that it was 'spiritual love and
union I offer'; she was praying that he might be freed
of bodily desire for her. Her Catholic faith was a new
buttress against the poet; she was judicially separated but
not divorced from her husband. The 'spiritual union' was
at moments intense; she wrote to him on July 26 of that
year of an astral meeting she had experienced:

> 'You had taken the form I think of a great serpent, but
> I am not quite sure. I only saw your face distinctly &
> as I looked into your eyes (as I did the day in Paris you
> asked me what I was thinking of) & your lips touched
> mine. We melted into one another till we formed only
> one being, a being greater than ourselves who felt all
> & knew all with double intensity . . .'

She was at pains to point out that there was nothing physical in the union: 'Material union is but a pale
shadow compared to it.'

The spirit world still drew him. Progressing through
the various stages of the Golden Dawn, he was also
turning more and more towards the help of mediums,
attending séances all over London, often in a spirit of
hope rather than expectation.

A new *Collected Works,* subsidized by the faithful Annie
Horniman, was published in 1908. Augustus John came
to Coole to sketch him for an etching. Despite his increasingly acknowledged eminence – when Swinburne

died there was talk of his being appointed poet laureate
– Yeats felt himself to be a detached figure. His relations
with his family were not relaxed. His home was still a
set of rooms in Woburn Buildings, more of them now,
and more comfortably furnished, but not a permanent
home. Coole and its chatelaine, so important to him,
suddenly became a fragile thing when Lady Gregory
suffered a stroke in February 1909. Already she was no
longer owner of the house, which had passed to Robert
when he reached twenty-one; knowing its preciousness
to her he let her retain it, but Yeats knew well that she was
his passport to its seven woods, its comforts, its library and
wine cellar. The young Gregory was inclined to feel that
the poet made himself too much at home and took his
welcome rather too much for granted. At this time too,
Yeats's friend Synge was gravely ill and died on March
24. He was only thirty-eight. Yeats was conscious of his
own age, of life moving on, of mortality. Quite early his
lustrous dark hair became shot with grey, and by 1910
his poems are beginning to refer to himself as if he were
older than his actual forty-five years.

  A little group of poems written around the end of 1908,
including the 'No Second Troy' already quoted, mark his
tempered view of Maud Gonne; she is described in noble terms but in the past tense: 'she had fiery blood When
I was young', and he himself has a new confidence, 'I have
come into my strength, And words obey my call.' The
man of letters had survived the onslaught of the man of
action and could feel some vindication for his own life,

his own chosen path. The poems of *The Green Helmet and Other Poems,* of 1910, have a sense of hard-won, hard-mouthed achievement; the poet has steered himself through some stormy channels to reach this point. There is a new, sharp, aphoristic quality in some poems only four or half a dozen lines long. In thought, in diction, in his concept of what poetry was for and could do, he was on the move, just as, around him, events were building, gathering, combining in patterns that shifted and yet always grew. Confident empires were about to shake and break; certainties of every kind would be tested to the root. A new time was coming. The century, ten years old, was assuming its own momentum. Many poets would be left behind by that wave, bobbing in its wake as helpless as jellyfish. Yeats sensed and saw it, rose and rode with it, his mouth filled with its brine and blood, and was swept on with its wrecking front towards its unforeseeable end.

In 1910 there was a Parliamentary crisis at Westminster, between a Liberal government in the House of Commons, and a Tory majority in the House of Lords. With only a small government majority, the votes of the Irish members were crucial, and for the first time since the 1880s, the issue of Home Rule became a real one. At this critical time, it was announced that W.B. Yeats had become a member of the new British Academy of Letters, the only Irish writer among the thirty; and later he was also informed of the £150 annual government pension. Welcome as this was to Yeats, it caused controversy in Dublin and again his Nationalist convictions were questioned: he was 'Pensioner Yeats' to the wits. Although he made gestures towards the Nationalists, as when in 1911 he declined to make a speech in honour of Edward Gordon Craig, in London, when he found it would also involve proposing a toast to King George V, he remained a suspect figure. The tensions created by the award of the pension are illuminated by the only real quarrel Yeats and Augusta Gregory had. She was asked by Sir Edmund Gosse, Librarian to the House of Lords, Yeats's friend, and instigator of the award, to produce material to support the request, then wrote her an offensive letter telling her not to interfere. Lady Gregory, deeply offended, expected Yeats to make a robust reply on her behalf. When he failed to do so, she felt badly let down. He took refuge in being an artist unwise to the ways of the official world.

In this year his uncle George, to whom he had become increasingly close, died. George Pollexfen had shared Yeats's fascination with the psychic and mystic, and as a high-ranking Freemason was buried with full Masonic honours in a ceremony which Yeats observed with keen interest and appreciation. Lily Yeats, who had been in Sligo, heard the banshee wail before her uncle's death.

There were continuing difficulties with Annie Horniman. Her devotion had been to Yeats and Literature rather than to Ireland, and she now wanted to stop her subsidy to the Abbey. She offered to sell the theatre, which she effectively owned, to her co-directors, Lady

Gregory and Yeats. His workload as administrator of the theatre was meanwhile much reduced by the appointment in 1910 of Lennox Robinson, a young playwright from Cork, as manager. Robinson was well suited to the job and was to become the Abbey's Director, but in that year, on the death of King Edward VII, he incurred Miss Horniman's fury by failing to close the theatre as part of the national mourning. Miss Horniman blamed Yeats and Lady Gregory, and there was a falling-out. Miss Horniman was bought out, after a scramble to assemble enough money, and Yeats lost his patron and unpaid secretary. The Abbey, however, survived, with Yeats still the moving spirit, much to Maud Gonne's disapproval. With an almost proprietorial view of his poems as his and her 'children', she scolded him for devoting time to the mundane business of theatre management instead of writing more verses. During late 1911 and early 1912, the Abbey company engaged in a controversial tour of America, where the 'Playboy' aroused stormy reactions from Irish-American audiences, and on one occasion the entire company was taken into police custody in Philadelphia, until the ever-helpful John Quinn arranged bail. Lady Gregory was with them on this stressful tour; in Maud's view she and Yeats had the Abbey as an all-too demanding child. Yeats continued his whole-hearted involvement, establishing an acting school to help resolve the chronic lack of suitable actors and evolve the theatre's own style.

For some time Yeats, in London, had been friendly with a young American poet who had deposited himself firmly

in the in many ways rather complacent and somnolent
London literary scene. This was Ezra Pound, confident,
disrespectful, brimful of intelligence and opinions,
contemptuous of the past and an apostle of the new, he
had given the new kind of poetry he admired a name,
Imagism. Like an explorer surveying Conan Doyle's
Lost World, Pound's eyes swept over the poetic landscape of London, its dinosaurs and extinct volcanoes, its
tigers and jackals, before picking out its most vital large
denizen. He applied himself to W.B. Yeats, who found
him entertaining, often annoying, but undoubtedly
stimulating. He had met no-one like Pound, who was
indeed something of a one-off, at least in the field of poetry. Pound was the lover, and later the husband, of Olivia
Shakespear's daughter Dorothy, and so became part of
Yeats's extended and anucleic 'family'. He and Dorothy
referred to Yeats as 'The Eagle'. Yeats also met and was
much influenced by Rabindranath Tagore, the Bengali
poet living in London, and was even more influenced by
the 'rediscovery' in 1911 of John Donne, which signalled
the new ascendancy of the seventeenth-century English
poets over the eighteenth- and nineteenth-century masters who until recently had dominated the scene.

Such new contacts pricked at his restlessness. He felt
himself capable of new poems, and his acquaintance with
younger people like Ezra and his friends, and Maud's
daughter Iseult, now eighteen and at least as beautiful as
her mother, made him feel strongly that he did not wish
to be regarded as the poet of a bygone era, but as one

still creative, still making new discoveries. In self-belying fashion he wrote 'To a Child Dancing in the Wind',

> '. . . you are young,
> So we speak a different tongue.'

– a poem of foreboding for Iseult Gonne.

Although he had never attended university, Yeats in 1913 had serious discussions about the post of Professor of English at Trinity College. Dowden was ill and considering retirement. There was some support for his appointment; he was by now an experienced and successful lecturer, and had thought deeply about literature. In those days there was far less administrative work for professors to do. But Dowden decided to stay on. It was not Yeats's first flirtation with academia; in 1909 he had tried and failed to obtain a lectureship at University College, Dublin. At that time he was very much engaged in Dublin life and his mission for a national literature; he may have seen a position in either university as a good platform for this cause. By 1913 he was almost at the end of this phase.

The summer of 1913, at Coole, was disturbed by the arrival of a telegram from Mabel Dickinson, to inform her lover that she was pregnant. Yeats was horrified. He had neither the wish nor the intention to marry Mabel. The pregnancy turned out to be either a false alarm or a trap; Yeats believed the latter, and there followed a series of heated meetings in London before their affair

was finally abandoned. To Lady Gregory, the import
was that Yeats should find himself, or be found, a wife.

In 1914, the fruits of his latest thought were published
under the somewhat forbidding title of *Responsibilities.* Its
invocation to his ancestors asks their pardon that he has
nothing more to present to the long family line but books:

> 'Although I have come close on forty-nine,
> I have no child, I have nothing but a book,
> Nothing but that to prove your blood and mine.'

This matter was on his mind. Some of the poems in
the collection show a calm, absorbed mastery of Irish
mythic themes as if deliberately intended to show his
Sinn Fein opponents, literary and political, that he was
the master harpist whose gaze went beyond Ireland's
flesh and spirit, to the very soul. There is also the poem
of very contemporary reproof to the (unnamed) Lord
Ardilaun, 'To a Wealthy Man who promised a Second
Subscription to the Dublin Municipal Gallery if it were
proved the People wanted Pictures'. It draws on Yeats's
Italian visit and his knowledge of the great Renaissance
patrons of art to chide the beer baron for troubling
with what 'the blind and ignorant town' thought about
art. The poem leads into 'September 1913', a threnody
for his country's lost greatness of soul:

> 'Romantic Ireland's dead and gone,
> It's with O'Leary in the grave.'

The malicious impishness of George Moore continued to sting him. Verbal caricatures of Yeats had appeared in a number of Moore's works from the 1898 'Evelyn Innes' on. In the fictionalized memoir *Ave* he was memorably described as resembling 'a great umbrella forgotten by some picnic party'.

In January 1914 he was stung by an extract from a further Moore volume, *Vale*, in the English Review, poking mockery at his aristocratic connections and pretensions, and his collection of poems of that year begins and ends with a high-minded, but direct reply that asserts his own pride in his ancestors for what they were, and his ability to rise above the fact that:

> '. . . all my precious things
> Are but a post the passing dogs defile.'

Moore and his attack are not mentioned by name, but the put-down was as magisterial as any delivered by a satiric bard in the heroic age.

By the time *Responsibilities* was published, Britain and France were at war with Germany. The war showed King George's pensioner to be no sort of imperialist. He made no contribution to the flood of bombast and anti-German invective unloosed by the combat. His thoughts centred on Ireland. Home Rule, accepted by the Westminster Parliament, contested by militant Unionists in the North, had been abruptly shelved for the duration of the war with Germany. There was discontent, industrial struggle, a testing of strength between workers and owners, both Irish and English. Socialism and trade unionism were preached at urban street-corners. Yeats's sympathies, as also Maud's, lay in January 1914 with the locked-out workers of Dublin and their hungry families, in the bitter dispute provoked by the transport strike, and in this he found common ground with AE and many other writers. Another successful lecture tour in the United States took place in 1914. In New York he was reunited with his father. Yeats senior had gone with Lily to New York in 1908, when she was on a sales trip for Dun Emer products, and had simply stayed on, enjoying life in what was in many ways an Irish city, and surveying his talented progeny benevolently from afar. Occasionally he wrote peace-making letters when tantrums broke out.

He was also running up debts which Willie had to pay off. John Quinn, from whom Yeats had been estranged from some years in a somewhat ludicrous dispute in which Quinn thought, or saw, that Yeats was paying too much attention to his mistress (Yeats rather grandly responded that he might have sought to seduce Quinn's wife, if he had one, but that it was not gentlemanly to seduce another man's mistress: the callow boy who shrank from smutty talk had become a man of the world), now friends again with Yeats, kept a friendly eye on the old man. They believed that J.B. should be sent back to Ireland, to be cared for by Lily and Lolly. But the crafty artist, enjoying a Bohemian old age, would have none of it. Yeats's earnings from the American lectures enabled him to pay £500 back to Lady Gregory.

Yeats continued to divide his life between London and Ireland, still enjoying his summers at Coole. His interest in spiritualism had not grown less. Attendance between 1912 and 1914 at séances given by a young English medium, Elizabeth Radcliffe, who could go into a trance and produce 'automatic' (i.e. spirit-guided) writing in six or more different languages, including Greek and Hebrew, reinforced his belief in communication with the dead, and in our ability to tap into a metaphysical universe. He was increasingly obsessed by astrology and the science of forecasting, believing that certain actions or decisions were best taken at specific times as indicated by the positions of the constellations. By 1914 an Adeptus Theoricus Minor of the Degree 6=5 in the Order of the Golden Dawn, he made an initiate of a young woman who impressed him, and whom he was already considering as a possible candidate for the position of wife to Mr Yeats. This was Georgie Hyde-Lees. Again it was Olivia Shakespear who had been the means of introduction. Known to her family as 'Dobbs', she was clever, attractive, well-read and interested in the occult. The tide of Yeats's self-awareness was coiling back and he found himself contemplating his childhood years, finishing the study *Reveries of Childhood and Youth* at Christmas 1914; there was also a market for such reminiscences by the famous. The reader of this work will find the emphasis very different to that of a modern

biography of Yeats: his grandfather Pollexfen emerges as
the key figure in the young man's development as an
artist, a tribute to the immense importance of the Sligo
background, but also something more picturesque and
Irish than the streets of west London. Yeats was working
closely with Pound, particularly during the winters of
1914, 1915 and 1916, spent at a rented house in Sussex,
Stone Cottage. Pound was his amanuensis, or literary
secretary, assistance needed by Yeats in part because of
his poor eyesight and his wish not to strain his eyes,
but the job title does less than justice to the secretary's
influence on the older man. Pound wrote Yeats's letters
at Yeats's dictation, and read to Yeats, the matter rang-
ing from works on witchcraft and spells to the poetical
output of William Wordsworth. Often they discussed
and argued over literary matters. Pound was busy on his
own account as well, getting poems of Yeats's published
in the USA, preparing his own anthology of Imagist
verse, writing poems of his own. Yeats took up many of
Pound's suggestions about his own work both in poetry
and prose.

Despite his silence on the issues of the Great War, com-
pliments from the British establishment continued. In
December 1915 he told his sister Lily that he had been
offered, and declined, a knighthood. Maud Gonne
during this time remained in France and worked as a
nurse tending battlefield casualties, as did Iseult – Maud
far more than Yeats was troubled by the deaths, among
so many, of so many Irish soldiers. Removed from the

blood, gas and gangrene, he was able to bring even world war into the scheme of cycles of human development and the slow movement of the forces of destiny. His response 'On Being Asked for a War Poem' (as he was by Henry James, for an anthology to raise money for war charities, in February 1915) said:

> 'I think it better that in times like these
> A poet's mouth be silent . . . '

– but 1916 was to prove that it was not the times, but the issues, and the way they touched him, that prompted the poet's reactions.

The war left one legacy of action for Yeats in the campaign he waged with Lady Gregory to have Hugh Lane's French painting collection shown in the National Gallery in Dublin. Lane, a wealthy art dealer and a nephew of Lady Gregory's, was a victim of the torpedoing of the *Lusitania* in May 1915. He had planned to leave his fine French paintings to Dublin, but annoyed by the rejection of plans to build a new gallery, had switched the bequest to the National Gallery in London. When he was appointed Director of the Dublin National Gallery, he amended the will, but failed to have it witnessed. London refused to accept the codicil to Lane's will, and Lady Gregory, with Yeats's staunch support, battled for the rest of her life to have the pictures moved to Ireland. It was only in 1959, twenty years after the poet's death, that a compromise solution was agreed.

During their time together in Stone Cottage in the winter of 1915, Ezra Pound, pursuing his interest in Oriental themes, introduced Yeats to the classic Noh drama of Japan. Noh, which means 'accomplishment', is lyric drama, with dancing and a chorus, the whole noble in tone and sonorous in language. Not least among its points of interest for him was that the players were masked. Yeats seized on it, seeing in it another form of his old ideal of an 'aristocratic' literature. Influenced by what he learned, Yeats wrote a drama on Noh lines, 'At the Hawk's Well', the first of a set of 'Four Plays for Dancers', performed with masks and elaborately choreographed movement, to a decor and music supplied by the artist Edmund Dulac. The subject of the play was the quest for wisdom of the legendary Irish hero, Cuchulain, a favourite poetic character of Yeats's. Just three weeks after its inaugural performance in a grand London drawing room in April 1916, Yeats shared the general surprise and shock of the Easter Rising.

The men of action had struck. Padraig Pearse, Yeats's old literary adversary, had proclaimed the Irish Republic. John McBride, his one-time rival in love, was another of the leaders. After a week, the might of empire restored order and the status quo, but the destroyed buildings, the shell of the Post Office, remained as witnesses. The echo of the execution-squads' rifle-fire would not be stilled. Pearse, McBride and the others who were shot or jailed, had failed in their attempt to galvanize the country into a sudden, unstoppable national crusade. But the momentum of Easter 1916, though it built up slowly, became unstoppable in the end. Yeats's immediate reaction was distress and despair: he thought it a misjudgement of these men, 'poets and teachers', and a forlorn gesture. Deeply stirred by it, he let his thoughts lead him and came to the view that it was indeed a momentous event that would have profound effects. Throughout his lifetime, Irishmen had talked, argued, disagreed about the future of their own country. Now, out of blood, rubble, an uncompromising declaration, and emblematic deaths, there was a different feeling abroad. More must happen. Only a few days after the firing squads, he began work on his poem Easter 1916.

The English poet W.H. Auden was to comment that the cataclysm of 1914–1918 did not produce, from the ranks of English poets, a work to rival the poem written by W.B. Yeats on a small, failed revolt in a peripheral city of Europe. The men of the Rising had stepped out of and beyond 'the casual comedy' and been transformed: 'A terrible beauty is born'. Three times that much-debated line is repeated. Its juxtaposition of opposites, in that context, offers different meanings, and it is impossible to read it without hindsight. It seems prophetic in that the Rising led not only to independence but to civil war. But for Yeats the uppermost meaning was to express the dramatic and absolute nature of 'All changed, changed utterly' – these men, commonplace figures from daily life, had created something out of themselves that was, to borrow a phrase from another poet 'immortal diamond.'

After a short visit to Dublin, to see the evidence of the Rising for himself, Yeats travelled on to Colleville in Normandy, where Maud was living. Perhaps with the death of McBride and the Catholic Maud's new status as a widow, he asked her once again to marry him, to be once again refused. With McBride a martyr for Ireland, Maud's view of her detested and estranged husband had changed. She honoured his memory and proudly titled herself Madame Maud Gonne McBride. Now, however, Yeats asked her if she would agree to his proposing to Iseult, now aged twenty-one. When she was seventeen, she had jokingly said that she would marry him. Now he was serious. The year before, he had written a poem to her:

> 'My dear, my dear, I know
> More than another
> What makes your heart beat so.'
> ('To a Young Girl')

Maud agreed that he should ask. Iseult herself was nonplussed. She had had many male admirers, but she knew Yeats was someone special. In the end she could not respond at all, and he knew it was a failed venture. What prompted it? It is likely that Yeats was acting in accordance with what he took to be advice, or at any rate a favourable augury, from the unknown world of spirit. He was keen to marry, convinced that the timing was right in terms of his own horoscope and anxious not to be beaten by the astrological clock. Having in the past been published by a number of small publishers, some of whom had already gone out of business, he tidied up his literary affairs by employing a literary agent, and transferring his copyrights to Macmillan, of London, who would from now on be his publishers (except for the limited Cuala editions of certain works).

At the same time, still with the heightened sense of what it was to be Irish that followed April 1916, he wanted to establish a home in Ireland – a proper home for himself, rooted in the soil and history of the country. The place was already chosen, it was a semi-derelict tower and adjacent cottage at Ballylee, close to Coole Park. Lady Gregory was helpful in the details of the purchase. The property would need a great deal of work and expenditure to become a proper home, and the thought drove him to work. For Ballylee's chatelaine, he had not given up hopes of Iseult Gonne, although Georgie Hyde-Lees, as an alternative candidate, was also in his mind. He confided this to Lady Gregory. Georgie seemed far more suitable to Yeats's patron than Iseult. She shared Yeats's interest in the occult, admired his poetry, liked him personally; she came from an upper-middle-class milieu and had a modest but useful private income. Yeats returned to France to stay with Maud and Iseult, hopeful that proximity would have its effect. But for Iseult the poet, now aged fifty-one, the friend and admirer of her mother, with all his grave, ceremonious charm, his fame, the half-hidden glamour of his spiritual researches, was unimaginable as a husband. He returned from their household (with its dogs, birds, monkeys, rabbits and parrot) in company with them. Maud wanted to go on to Ireland but on her arrival in England was served with an official warrant forbidding her and Iseult to travel there. While Maud remained angrily in London, Yeats discussed the niceties of a marriage settlement with Mrs Tucker, the remarried mother of Georgie. Despite her mother's reservations, Georgie was keen to accept, and the engagement was announced in September 1916. Soon afterwards, Georgie was introduced to Maud. Although Maud spoke a little scathingly to others, to Yeats and his fiancée she behaved with great propriety and friendship. Iseult, too, was introduced to Georgie, the number two candidate, only three years older than herself.

Georgie, soon to be renamed George by her husband, was a level-headed person who knew what she was taking on. At the last minute, her mother turned against the idea and tried to enlist Lady Gregory's help to stop the marriage, but Lady Gregory felt that Georgie was the right person. She knew that the poet required a degree of care and cosseting that neither of the Gonne women would provide. The wedding took place in a London Registry Office on 20 October 1917, with Ezra Pound as Yeats's best man. The honeymoon was begun in a rather stiffly bourgeois hotel in the Ashdown Forest, a favourite part of England for Yeats, not far from Stone Cottage where he and Pound had worked. On their arrival, Yeats was assailed by terrible doubts about the whole thing. Whatever his feelings for his new wife, they were very different from the consuming passion for Maud, which by extension also included Iseult. An immense depression seized him, he felt ill, oppressed, believing that he had trapped himself in a situation that was false to everyone involved.

The marriage might have come to an abrupt end, or wasted itself in aridity, but for Mrs Yeats's resourcefulness. With skill and wisdom, she hit on the key to Yeats's citadel. It was not sex, or overt emotion, or recrimination of any kind. The recent recruit into the Order of the Golden Dawn, at this crucial and desperate moment of her own life, enlisted the aid of the spirit world to capture the Adept. Sitting in their over-furnished hotel room, she began to write, as if quite unconscious of what she was doing. The message was: 'With the bird all is well at heart. Your action was right for both.' To Yeats the import of this was perfectly clear. The all-knowing spirits had approved of his decision, and it was the right one for Maud and Iseult. The heavy depression lifted at once.

George's little trick — as she admitted it to be, after her husband's death — not only worked brilliantly, but formed the start of a long and extraordinary partnership. Yeats, always fascinated by apparent contact with the spirit world, always keen to investigate a new manifestation or a new medium, now found himself married to someone who was herself a medium of exceptional quality. He did not for one moment consider this to be a strange or improbable coincidence. Rather it was something inevitable, brought about by his long and painstaking attention to the spirit world. It was a vindication of the interest which many of his friends and colleagues mocked at. With such access to arcane knowledge, Yeats was transformed from his uneasy, neurotic, self-questioning condition into an ardent and vigorous spiritual researcher. Husband and wife were destined to spend thousands of hours at the table together, he asking questions, she recording in her 'automatic' writing the responses of a whole group of spirit communicators; and from this was to emerge, at last, Yeats's complete theory of life. It was also to make its mark very strongly in his poetry.

CHAPTER SEVEN

'*I*, THE POET WILLIAM YEATS'

What kind of man had the twenty-five year old George acquired as a husband? All accounts of Yeats state, as his photographic images affirm, that he was a handsome figure of a man. The English poet Richard Aldington, recording an occasion in 1913 when Yeats, on behalf of the Royal Society of Literature, presented an award to his fellow Irishman and mystic, James Stephens, noted:

'He spoke in his beautiful voice; he expressed Celtic love with his more beautiful face; he elevated and waved his yet more beautiful hands.'

– the ironic tone serves to underline the self-awareness of Yeats's appearance (the elegance of his hands was frequently remarked on). At this stage in his life he was a man of letters, a man of the theatre, a man with a penchant for social life (a later writer, Stanley Weintraub, referred to him as 'a lover of tailcoats and testimonial dinners'). But still and primarily he was 'the poet William Yeats'. What was most important to him was what happened inside his mind. He was not practical; it is unlikely that in his adult life Yeats ever picked up a dishcloth or attempted to mend a fuse. In the frequent removals from one rented house to another during his early married life, he took no part in the packing. He could take a high degree of attention for granted – the servants at Coole were irritated by the way in which he ignored them, holding out his teacup to be refilled as he talked on to fellow-guests without even looking up – and retained the youthful habit of chanting or mumbling lines that were in his head. He was physically fit and well. To a wife who was prepared to make of him her own life's work, he was, for ten years, an ideal husband. When he brought George to Ireland to meet his sisters, they noticed immediately how sleek and healthy he looked. He was not silent or reserved; he talked to her. The community of interests seemed perfect. It was not long before George became pregnant.

She shared his enthusiasm for the Ballylee project, and spent her own money on renovation work before she ever set foot there. They settled for a time in Oxford, where Yeats was able to use the resources of the Bodleian Library to help in his heightened interest in the visionary tradition. In February 1918 Robert Gregory, a major in the Royal Flying Corps, was killed in action, not by the enemy but accidentally by an Italian allied airman. His mother was deeply stricken, and Yeats, who had never had a close rapport with her son, responded to her grief rather than his own in two elegiac poems, 'The Shepherd and the Goatherd', and 'In Memory of Major Robert Gregory'. Robert's death was also the inspiration of 'An

Irish Airman Foresees His Death', written in that same
year, but here the personal element is removed, and in
fact the sentiments:

> 'Those that I fight I do not hate,
>   Those that I guard I do not love.'

— are most unlikely to have been Gregory's. His experience has been taken and transformed, into the beautiful
evocation of flight and aerial battle, and the explanation
of why he is there, sufficient for the pilot but, with its
repetition of the word 'waste', leaving the reader to
ponder the true human value of the driving 'lonely
impulse of delight.'

In the early summer of 1918 Lady Gregory lent the
Yeatses Ballinamantane House, in Gort, close to Coole
and to Ballylee, from where they could supervise the
work on the tower house. Not just the fabric of the
building but everything within was planned to be Irish,
and hand-made. It was a western refuge from a new
storm that was breaking to the east, as the British tried
to enforce conscription on the men of Ireland. In the
hope of avoiding confrontation, many leading figures
from the Republican movement were arrested, including Maud Gonne, who was sent to Holloway Prison in
London. Yeats and others agitated to have her released,
and after five months she was set free, but forbidden to
travel to Ireland. She moved to Yeats's rooms in Woburn
Buildings, while Yeats and George rented her Dublin

house at 73 St Stephen's Green. George had been very ill, and remained in poor health throughout her pregnancy.

On 11 November 1918, the Armistice was signed and warfare ceased. The restriction placed upon Maud Gonne was not lifted, and she made an illegal entrance, in disguise, to Ireland, turning up unexpectedly at her house. Yeats, concerned for George's health, would not even let her in. The exhausted and indignant Maud had to seek shelter elsewhere. As political events in Ireland moved to crisis point, with Sinn Fein candidates winning a majority of Irish seats in the post-war election, refusing to go to Westminster and (if not in jail) instead assembling the first Daíl Eireann in January 1919, Yeats's attention was focused on his family. His daughter Anne was born in Dublin at the end of February. Yeats's own hope, and also the forecast from George's automatic writing, had been for a boy. But he was delighted with the child.

That year he gave up his long tenancy of the London apartment in Woburn Buildings, and they moved to Ballylee. It was not intended as a permanent home but as a summer one, nor were all the works completed. It was to be their only peaceful summer there for some years to come. In October, as guerrilla war between the Sinn Fein government and the British was beginning, they moved back to Oxford; but in January they went to America, leaving the baby with Lily and Lolly. The need for money prompted this; Ballylee was consuming large sums, and the lifestyle of a middle-class family was considerably more expensive than that of a literary

bachelor. Yeats arranged with Quinn for a heavy programme of lectures and readings over four months, that
would take him right across North America.

America to Yeats appears to have been mainly a re-
source to boost his bank balance. It did not arouse in him
the friendly if satirical kind of analysis that W.H. Auden
would later apply to it, or the enthusiasm of Robert Louis
Stevenson at an earlier date. It was a land, as Oscar Wilde
had observed, that prided itself on democracy, equality
and informality, which had a diminishing appeal to Yeats
in the first two cases, and a negative one in the last. The
Irish Americans, sentimental in their regard for the old
country, ignorant of much that was happening and even
more so of the older past, supporters of Sinn Fein rather
than Union, did not appeal to him, though they filled
halls in large numbers to listen to the beautiful voice
chant the lines of 'Innisfree'. In Portland, Oregon, Yeats
received a gift from an unexpected source. Junzo Sato,
the Japanese Consul there, an enthusiast of his poetry,
presented him with a ceremonial sword in an embroi-
dered silk sheath. It was more than five hundred years
old: 'Chaucer had not drawn breath When it was forged'
('My Table'). Yeats kept the sword on the table in his
study, its potency as a symbol further enhanced for him
by its craftsmanship and lineage.

America was also the chosen homeland of John Butler
Yeats, now eighty years old, happy, ebullient and improvi-
dent as ever. Despite frequent pleas from Lily and Lolly,
he showed not the least inclination to leave New York

for Dublin or anywhere else. Once again his son paid
off his debts, and the old man and his daughter-in-law
took a liking to each other. With John Quinn, Yeats attended a rally in New York for Eamon de Valera, who
was also on tour in the USA, raising support and funds
for the embattled Sinn Fein and the Irish Republic. This
was his first experience of the future Taoiseach and first
President of Ireland, and Yeats judged him, with no great
originality, to be a desiccated figure, 'a living argument
rather than a living man'.

On their return from America, first to London, then to
Oxford, events in Ireland again claimed Yeats's attention,
though again, they were personal rather than political. In
marrying him, George had been fully aware that she was
taking on much of his baggage, not least his continuing
close friendship with the Gonnes, and she adapted to this
by making friends with Iseult. Maud, more than twenty
years her elder, and with Yeats at her feet since 1889, was
friendly too, but more distant. Iseult had shared the Yeatses' very first Christmas together, only two months after
their marriage. At the daily or twice-daily automatic
writing sessions that were a dominant feature of his life
with George, Yeats's questions about Maud and Iseult
were frequent. While they showed George the extent
of his continuing obsession with them, it enabled her,
through the Controls and Communicators who drove
her pen, to help keep them in their place. Despite the
barring-out of Maud, and the sharpening of their political divergence as the independence conflict grew, their

ties remained strong. Iseult, whose virginity had been claimed by the sexually rapacious Ezra Pound, and who for a short time had been his mistress, married a young aspiring poet from Ulster, Francis Stuart, only eighteen and uncontrollably wild and wayward in attitude and behaviour. Iseult, soon pregnant, was beaten up regularly, deprived of food and sleep, her clothes were burned. Her mother's desperation, communicated to Yeats, resulted in a trip by him to Dublin, which helped to patch things up for a time.

The poems to Robert Gregory were included in a collection published in 1919, *The Wild Swans at Coole*. Many other poems in the collection show an elegiac and reflective note, including the beautiful title poem, written in October 1916, contrasting his present heart-sore state with the lightness of spirit he had experienced nineteen years before when he saw the swans at Coole for the first time. His own ageing and Maud Gonne's grey hairs are not spared. The suite of seven poems, *Upon a Dying Lady*, refer to Mabel Beardsley, sister of his brief collaborator of the 1890s, Aubrey. She was dying of cancer, and her gaiety of spirit though assailed by ravaging disease made a profound impression on Yeats. But the later poems, written when he and his new wife were already sharing long hours in communication with the unseen world, sound a different note and signal a reactivated interest in the psychic and supernatural. 'The Phases of the Moon' from 1919 brings back two figures from his earlier imaginings, Michael Robartes and Owen

Aherne. Tramping the road past the poet's tower with
its one lamplit window, they discuss him (in a way that
foreshadows a very different Irish writer, Flann O'Brien,
in *At Swim-Two-Birds):*

> '. . . now he seeks in book or manuscript
> What he shall never find.'

To Yeats, after decades of reading, it was apparent now
that the truths he sought were not to be found in a library,
but by direct contact with the wisdom of the spirits. As
his two wandering sages go on to recount the phases of
the moon and their ineluctable impalpable influence on
humanity, the poet himself is pondering on human types,
Hunchback, Saint, Fool, who recur in some of the other
poems in the collection.

These themes are continued in the poems of *Michael
Robartes and the Dancer* of 1921. George Yeats is present in
these poems where women ask and answer impenetrable
questions, or cry out at night in strange voices, and dream
vivid, emblematic dreams. She is specifically addressed
in the apologetic 'Under Saturn', where, though unable
to forget the 'lost love, inseparable from my thought
Because I have no other youth', he expresses gratitude
for 'the wisdom that you brought, The comfort that you
made'. This collection also includes the poems inspired
by the Easter Rising and written five years earlier, bringing the imagery of 'Easter 1916' close to that of the
poem which, for many, is one of the key poems, perhaps

the most revelatory poem, of the spirit of the twentieth
century, 'The Second Coming'. Almost centrally placed
in Yeats's long poetic career, it is central to the progress
of his thought. Some of its themes look backwards. The
image of the rough beast harks back to an early vision in
a Golden Dawn séance. The 'widening gyre' represents
a fundamental image of his developing thought – the
gyre is a cone-form, the cosmos can be represented by
two interlocked and spinning cones. As one waxes, the
other wanes. But as it waxes, it weakens, the movement
slows, in the end the opposite cone will gain momentum
and, from its apex, its energy will expand and prevail, as
part of a cycle whose process occupies two thousand
years. Yeats saw these gyres as endowed with distinct and
opposed qualities, which he labelled as Objectivity and
Subjectivity. He believed that the two thousand years of
the Christian era had formed an Objective stage of the
process, and were about to end in a disintegration which
would mark the beginning of twenty centuries of a Subjective epoch. Catastrophe and chaos marked the ending
of these epochs, and the transference of expansive power
to the cone of Subjectivity foretold a time of disunion,
violence, selfishness and destructiveness. 'The Second
Coming' shows Yeats at his full power as a poet-mage; a
few months later, 'A Prayer for My Daughter' shows the
poet-father, back on earth, with thoughts of upbringing
and future husbands for the three-month-old child. It
is a poem much lambasted by latter-day feminists, with
its 'be good, sweet maid, and let who will be clever' at-

titude to female education. Yeats may well have had this
as a general view. His comments on women in politics
are notably caustic. At the Cuala Press, where his sister
Lolly did all the work, he was most reluctant to allow
her any responsibility in the choice of books, regarding
that as his own prerogative.

Encouraged by messages in the 'automatic writing',
the Yeatses sought quickly to have another child. During
the summer of 1920, George suffered a miscarriage. In
October Yeats went to Dublin again, this time to have his
tonsils removed by Oliver St John Gogarty. Prior to the
operation, he stayed at a house Maud Gonne had bought,
at Glenmalure in the Wicklow Mountains. Her son, Sean
McBride, by then a student, had already identified himself
firmly with the republicans. By this time the auxiliary
'Black and Tan' police had been introduced. Maud's
house was raided, not for the last time, and she berated
Yeats in letters for not doing more to prevent the activities of these legalized terrorists. Yeats continued to be
more concerned with his growing concept of cosmic
history, though he did make an impassioned speech at
the Oxford University Union in favour of Irish self-
government (the motion was carried by a large majority).

He was writing a further volume of autobiography in
1921, dealing with his twenties, *The Trembling of the Veil,*
and, like the preceding books, chiefly concerned with
his artistic development rather than forming any kind
of consistent record of his life. On August 22 of that
year his son Michael was born; they were now renting

a house in the old town of Thame, between Oxford and London. This time the spirit forecasters had been more circumspect, but Yeats himself had been confident it would be a boy. Now he had more to offer his ancestors than books – the Yeats name was preserved into a further generation. He speculated on whether his old uncle, Isaac Yeats, might leave some of his 'treasures' to be passed on through future generations of the family (Jack and his wife Cottie were childless, the sisters unmarried). Against this positive event, the descent of Ireland into civil war caused him great distress; after the narrow Dáil majority in favour of the Treaty vote in January 1922, it was plain that bloodshed would follow. Yeats was a supporter of the Treaty, believing the twenty-six-county 'Free State' to be the best option available. His brother Jack took the opposite view (as did Maud), supporting the Sinn Fein concept of a complete and independent republic; this resulted in an estrangement of the two brothers, a common happening in families throughout the land at this time.

In February, J.B. Yeats died in New York, aged eighty-three. He had retained his vigour and spirit to the last, and Willie felt that his father had made a good end. Lily and Lolly, who had kept a room ready for the old man's often-promised but never-accomplished return, were more distressed; particularly Lily, who felt her life had been a long imprisonment with her ill-tempered sister. They were surprised and pleased when their English sister-in-law appeared at this time in Dublin and set about buying a family house.

In the depressed atmosphere of civil war, property prices were low. George got a fine house in Merrion Square and organized the move. At last, Yeats, the doyen of Irish poets, had a permanent home in his own country, and right in the heart of the capital. Although the initiative had been George's, it was his arrival. When the summer came they moved to the tower, now called Thoor Ballylee, and settled happily, with Yeats still at work on *The Trembling of the Veil,* and Lady Gregory in residence close by at Coole Park and busy on her own memoirs. Soon the war caught up with them as the official government and the Republicans fought in bitter, bloody skirmishes, bombed bridges and houses, and shot known or suspect opponents in reprisal killings. Yeats was no longer surveying events from afar; they were all around. Any day might bring a Black and Tan or an IRA troop to his door. His *Meditations in Time of Civil War* were written at this time, during the sunny, murderous summer of 1922. They were published first, not in any Irish periodical but in the *London Mercury*.

In December 1922 his commitment to Ireland and to the Free State government was acknowledged when he was appointed by William Cosgrave, President of the Free State, to the Senate. His friend and doctor Gogarty was also a member. In Gogarty's view, Yeats was appointed not for his latter-day eminence but because long ago he had been admitted to the Irish Republican Brotherhood. Yeats saw it differently. He supported the founding of the Free State but had no party flag to brandish; he was representing only himself. Nevertheless he was taking a substantial risk. Every member of the Dáil, and especially those in government, was at risk of assassination. Gogarty was to be kidnapped in October 1923 and only his courage, strength and luck enabled him to escape an otherwise inevitable death by the gun. In January 1923 the government ordered the arrest of Maud Gonne, who had lost none of her fire; but Yeats's torments were behind him; he was as entrenched in his point of view as she. The spiritual union held, and there was no estrangement between them as there was with his brother.

An honorary doctorate from Trinity College, at almost the same time as his appointment to the Senate, also greatly pleased Yeats. From now on he was Dr Yeats; the boy who had shrunk from exposing his ignorance to the university was now one of its honoured members. Earlier in the same year, Queen's University, Belfast, had also awarded him an honorary doctorate: a reminder, from the still-British six counties, that that self-segregated part of Ireland could also honour him and in so doing claim him as, in part, their own.

George's purchase of the big Merrion Square house also provided a new home for the Cuala Press. The Yeats sisters, pursuing their avocations with industry and integrity, made little profit and earned little themselves. The business ran on an overdraft. When Lily fell ill with suspected tuberculosis, Willie and George stepped in; she was sent to a nursing home in England; the press and the embroidery business were installed in the Yeats basement.

The award to Yeats of the Nobel Prize for Literature, in November 1923, came with utter unexpectedness; the canvassing and media speculation of later years was then unknown. He was informed through the *Irish Times,* and its editor, Robert Smyllie, recorded his reaction: '. . . to my amazement the only question he asked was, "How much, Smyllie, how much?" ' The sum was £7,000, by far the largest single sum Yeats was to earn.

In December Dr Yeats and his wife travelled to Stockholm to be guests of honour in a series of parties and ceremonies which included a royal reception by the King of Sweden. He lectured to the Royal Swedish Academy on the Irish Theatre, and saw a production, more sumptuous than anything the Abbey could have mustered, of 'Cathleen ni Houlihan'. His prize was also seen as an international recognition of a renascent Ireland; there was no doubt that it was as an Irish writer that the Nobel selectors had chosen him, despite his English links; without the move to Dublin, the prize might well have gone elsewhere.

With Lennox Robinson in command, the Abbey Theatre was less demanding on Yeats's time and energies than it had been, but its continuing commitment to literary merit and innovation, at a time when stormy politics had given way to outright warfare in Ireland, and both sides took the view that 'those who are not with us are against us', made it vulnerable. In February 1926, Sean O' Casey's 'The Plough and the Stars', dealing ten

years on with the Easter Rising, would arouse a furore
at least as great as that started by 'The Playboy of the
Western World', and this time lead to threats to blow
up the theatre.

With Yeats's national and international honours, and his
own sociability, and an accomplished hostess in George,
their house became a social centre, on a scale wider than
his London 'Mondays', for his standing in Dublin was
comparatively much greater, and he was a political as
well as a literary and social figure. If to a large section
of the community he was tarnished by his adherence to
the Free State, to those who shared his political views
he was all the more valuable.

In 1924 he was nearing sixty, very much a successful
public man. But his health was not good, and in November George organized a long holiday in Italy. In the
Norman-Byzantine buildings of Sicily Yeats found with
enthusiasm later forms of the beautiful and hieratic mosaics he had seen before in Ravenna with Lady Gregory. In
January 1925 he met Ezra Pound for the first time in
five years. Pound had long abandoned London for
Paris; now he was about to begin his lengthy residence in
Italy. They moved on to Capri where Yeats finished work
on the first version of his prose work *A Vision,* his great
effort to translate the answers of George's spirit communicators, and his own gradually evolved views, into
a coherent system. He dedicated it to 'Vestigia', a name
for Moina Bergson, the wife of his one-time mentor in
the Golden Dawn, MacGregor Mathers. Yeats was always

to think with some affection of Mathers, summoning his
memory in a poem of 1920, 'All Souls' Night':

> 'I thought him half a lunatic, half knave,
> And told him so, but friendship never ends,'

(Mathers had died in 1918.) They progressed to Rome,
where Yeats, with the spiritual world temporarily off his
mind, spent much time thinking about contemporary
Italian political thought. It was early in the time of
Mussolini, Italy's political strong man whose dictatorial
rule through the Fascist Party was to prevail until the
country's military and political collapse in 1943.

Coming from a bitterly divided country that lived
under martial law and the ever-present terrorism, Yeats
looked at the Italian situation with great interest. It was
within his own lifetime that Italy had become a unified
state. Political factionism had weakened it; now under
the rule of a strong man, it appeared to be confident
and resurgent. Yeats's reading of Nietszche, prompted
by his friend John Quinn (who had died in 1924) had
given him the concept of the super-man. In the General Election of 1919, Yeats had seen how a democratic
process did not necessarily lead to a peaceful solution of
a country's problems. Whether it was the crowd in the
Abbey, howling against a play they disapproved of; or a
crowd in the street letting its passions be aroused by cheap
oratory, he had come to mistrust the popular will. The
poet who ruled the policies of the Abbey Theatre had

a pronounced dictatorial streak; he sought to impose rather than to persuade. This made him sympathetic to the strong man of Cosgrave's government, the Justice Minister, Kevin O'Higgins, who became a close friend.

Politically, Yeats had become conservative and authoritarian. In part it was a response to conditions in his own country. He believed it was necessary, but his views went beyond expediency. However, he remained absolutely faithful to his long-held principle of artistic liberty. Seeing the tide of religiously inspired repression rising in Ireland, he feared for what it would do. He spoke against the censorship of books such as Shaw's *The Black Girl In Search of God,* and against the bill to ban divorce. He was chagrined to see Irish freedom used to limit artistic and social freedom in Ireland. As his passionate speech on the divorce issue shows, he believed strongly that the element of Irish Protestantism, of which he was part on both sides of his family, had been a vital one in the growth of modern Irish culture and the emergence of a free Ireland, and he saw with concern how it was being stifled. It was not merely the burnings of grand country houses and the departure to England of many of the wealthy aristocracy, much as the traditionalist and lover of ceremony in Yeats deplored these things. The pluralism of Ireland in his view had been a strength, and the drive towards a Catholic state discouraged him. Despite his respect for the traditions of the Irish people, he had no great opinion of the 'Catholic peasantry', as shown in numerous exchanges in his letters with those who shared his view.

In the autumn of 1925 he returned to Italy, to muse once again in the majestic dim arcades of the San Ambrogio basilica in Milan. *A Vision* was published in London in January 1926, to a deafening silence from the press, apart from a friendly but somewhat baffled review by his old friend AE. In February Yeats found himself for the second time facing a yelling mob from the stage of the Abbey, on the opening night of O'Casey's 'The Plough and the Stars'. His words of angry scorn were totally inaudible, but he had taken the precaution of giving the *Irish Times* an advance copy, so that its memorable words:

'Is this to be an ever-recurring celebration of the arrival of Irish genius? Synge first, and then O'Casey!'

– were spread across the nation. Yeats taunted the rioters with the fact that their protest would merely serve to establish the playwright's name: '...the fame of O'Casey is born here tonight. This is his apotheosis.'

In 1926 he was also doing the state some service by presiding over the design of the country's new coinage, which was to provide the Free State with a handsome and aesthetically appealing coinage which, while following the sizes and denominations of the British, forsook imperial pomposity for the animals and birds of farm and countryside.

The summer of 1926, spent at Thoor Ballylee, was taken up by reading and writing. Yeats's health was not good. He was overweight, suffered from asthmatic attacks, and developed a hernia. George, careful of him as always, became concerned. He was busy finishing an adaptation of Sophocles' 'Oedipus Rex' for the Abbey, a successful production which would be followed by 'Oedipus at Colonnus', which he completed in the spring of 1927.

In July of that year he was horrified and shaken by the assassination of Kevin O'Higgins. Maud Gonne's son Sean McBride was among those arrested in the aftermath. At Maud's request, he tried to arrange for her to see her son in prison, but even the senatorial influence could not manage this. The beleaguered government had no favours to give to Madame Gonne McBride.

CHAPTER EIGHT

'THE SYSTEM'

Mrs George Yeats's 'automatic script', still preserved, amounts to 3,600 pages, written in 450 sessions within a period of twenty months. Such a quantity of writing reflects the intensity with which her husband, through her passive contact with 'Controls' and 'Communicators', interrogated the invisible and intangible entities who drove her hand. Even after her contacts for automatic writing fell silent, she was liable to talk in her sleep, her alert husband noting what was said, and the tones in which the utterance was made. Even before Yeats brought her into the fold of the Golden Dawn, George had been interested in the occult, though there was nothing to show that she was a particularly gifted medium. Brenda Maddox, in her study of the Yeats marriage, *George's Ghosts,* based on examination of the automatic writing, among other sources, came to the same conclusion as others already had, that the writings were made up. While others had made this assertion through scepticism or disbelief, she had observed through the scripts that the comments, injunctions and statements they contain can be read as a shrewd and clever manipulation of the inquiring poet's state of mind, by a wife who understood the rites and systems of occult inquiry, and who wanted nothing more than to encourage his genius, keep him happy, and maintain the focus of his devotion and attention firmly on herself. In all this she succeeded. Maddox states, 'My firm conviction is that at all times during the Automatic Script – even when four or five 'Controls' are recorded as gathered there at the same time – there were only two people in the room.'

It was noted that George was never willing to admit outside observers to those sessions. Yeats himself was entirely convinced of the authenticity of his wife's contacts and never appears to have questioned it. He was not a gullible type. In some respects he was notably hard-headed, as in his management of his own literary affairs and those of the Abbey Theatre. Like many intelligent people who cling to a quirky belief, he could semi-humorously emphasize it to excite or disarm sceptics, and some of his fairy visions may partake of this gently mischievous intention. But in this area he could not avoid the trap which awaits all seekers after the intangible and unprovable. His quest for occult knowledge was driven by the belief that there was something there to be known. Such a belief could not be founded upon objective proofs; but ways might be found to establish such proofs. Intuitions and insights might be valuable here. Rituals and special preparations like costumes and incense might help to create the necessary receptivity in the dull, physical brain (in one poem Yeats calls it 'inanimate'). In common with many contemporaries like the American psychologist William James, Yeats also experimented with – or enjoyed – such hallucinatory drugs as hashish and mescalin. He was certain that the key to contact with the non-physical world existed, and was there to be found. In these pursuits he was as earnest as his contemporary Albert Einstein was in working out the formula of the Theory of Relativity, though Yeats's metaphysical cosmos had nothing to do with mathematics. To this end he pursued many leads and was always aware that they were likely to prove to be dead ends. Once in France, he and Maud, who was by then converted to Roman Catholicism, went to a remote country place where drops of blood were said to well out from a painting of Christ. The swabs taken from the canvas, subjected to scientific analysis in London, proved to be not blood at all. To Yeats it was another false lead, but no more a disproof of his basic conviction than, in his favourite country pastime of angling, an unproductive cast would prove that fish did not exist. He was one of those, who, when the Society for Psychical Research (of which he was a member) finally proclaimed Madame Blavatsky to be a fraud and showed how she rigged her séances, was still ready to believe that there was some real insight there and that the lady had succumbed to the use of artificial aids in order to give her visions more objective reality; rather than to fake them absolutely.

A Vision, the book in which Yeats sought to express the structure and function of the non-physical world, was, in a sense, a continuous work in progress. Ever a reviser of his own work, he returned to *A Vision* as his researches continued and the final version of 1937 was substantially different to the first edition, published in January 1926. His cosmology is set forth in this work, which Yeats regarded as his most important, in prose at least, but which remains the least read of his major works. In the first edition, he went to some trouble in order not to identify his wife as the source of much of its content. This was at her own request: when later he was to reveal the part she had played, in *A Packet for Ezra Pound*, she was distressed and angry.

By November 1917, very soon after his marriage and the discovery of George's talent as a medium, the basis of the book was worked out. It was not his first attempt to set down his beliefs and perceptions. For as long as he could remember, Yeats had been involved in an inner dialogue, discussing ideas, events, interpretations and their renderings into verse with himself. He was conscious of this as a duality and inner conflict. It contributed strongly to the image of the mask frequently found in his writing, where one aspect of personality cloaks another. Productive as this was in his own creative work, he often found it troubling, and an obstacle to any true self-awareness. Between 1912 and 1914, he was an assiduous attender at London séances, including Elizabeth Maddox's sessions of automatic writing. It was during that time, from an American medium living in London, Mrs Wreidt, that he received his first communication from an astral spirit who introduced himself as Leo Africanus, a historical personage who had been an explorer and, geographers discovered, a poet. Yeats, who was always keen to communicate his enthusiasms, told another medium of this, and Leo began to speak to him through her also. He said he was Yeats's opposite self, the antithesis to Yeats's over-cautiousness and conscience, and that by association with Leo, Yeats would become a more complete individual. This gave double pleasure to Yeats, at once freeing him from the dualism that had seemed to be locked within him, and establishing a contact with the spirit world in which he was so keen to believe. These exchanges with Leo Africanus were made by letter, Yeats writing on his own behalf, and also transcribing the responses relayed through the medium. Leo, with an assured command of English, a language he was unlikely to have acquired during his earthly existence, called himself the poet's Interlocutor, 'hard & keen like a hunting animal, & now for your good & my own, I have chosen to linger near ...' Leo also hinted at a god-like spirit, 'remote & silent', and, questioned by Yeats as to whether he was image (of the poet's own imagination) or phantom (an external being), somewhat teasingly confessed to being both. In a short book, *Per Amica Silentia Lunae* ('In the Friendly Silence of the Moon') Yeats explores some of his own earlier experiences and broods on the concept of the Daimon as something that seeks its own opposite.

Despite occasional moments of vision or enlightenment, Yeats knew himself not be a visionary. Laborious ritual, or drugs, could bring him visions, but he knew that, unlike William Blake, he would never simply walk down a street and see a tree crowded with angels. He put some of the obliquities of his dialogue with Leo Africanus down to this:

'I am not convinced that in this letter there is one sentence that has come from beyond my imagination . . . I have been conscious of no sudden illumination.'

He was referring to a letter from Leo that he had just written down at the medium's dictation. But he added, 'I am confident now as always that spiritual beings if they cannot write and speak can always listen.'

A spirit named 'Leo' was to recur in the automatic writing sessions, and like Leo Africanus, one not sympathetic to Yeats. Leo was one of what the Yeatses called the 'Frustrators', spirits who sought to subvert the dialogue between George and the 'Communicators'. There were other elements in his wife's automatic script which Yeats recognized from previous communications through other mediums. Again he regarded this as only natural. The fact that he had talked about them to George at various times before their marriage did not mean that he would dream of their re-use in an innocent and well-intentioned plagiarism on her part.

The essential components of Yeats's cosmos are a far-off and uncommunicating God, a hierarchy of spirits, some of them angelic, others the souls of the human dead, and a structured progression of spirit towards a state of beatitude. The lower spirits, at least, are still engaged in a process of development; they are not entirely free from their attachment to the physical world (hence our ability to communicate with them, if we are sensitive enough). Earth itself, and the life it harbours, at the lowest end of the spectrum of being, is completely governed by its own external forces of sun, moon and the constellations. These can be analysed, set down, and partially understood. He and George spent many hours ascribing human types, and individual humans of note, to the 'houses' formed by the twenty-eight phases of the moon as it waxes, achieves fullness, and wanes again, reproducing as it does the long journey from the extreme of Objectivity, babyhood, to that of Subjectivity, the fool. Good and Evil as absolutes do not play a part in this cosmology; good effects and evil ones arise from every phase.

This is true of the great gyres whose two-thousand-year cycle of mutually involved and perpetual motion he sees both as containing the entire system and forming elemental parts of it, tiny polarities within the two vast alternating polarities of Subjective and Objective. Yeats noted that the metaphor or reality of the overlapping cones could include Man and Woman, Father and Mother. A further element was the existence of a messianic figure at the start of each two-thousand-year phase; to Yeats, who could not altogether escape the Christian tradition, Christ was the herald of the now-ending Objective era. He flirted with the thought that a child of his own might perform the role for the next, as though he and George were to be a Faust and Helen producing a more successful Euphorion.

Yeats's beliefs have puzzled many of his readers. At the root of this bafflement is a reluctance to accept that such dubious and eccentric notions, hard to separate from the florid charlatanry which is all most people see in psychic pursuits, could really be what Yeats believed in. To the Dublin populace he was 'Willie the Spooks'. He was not the first poet to talk to spirits: William Blake was his most obvious predecessor, but Blake was a most unworldly man, and if not slightly mad, certainly deeply unconventional.

William Yeats was a man of the world, courtly and ceremonious in his own style, and with a liking for the comforts of life. However tawdry some of the sideshows of psychism might be, none of Yeats's spiritual thought was cheap, or accepted without question, or assumed for show. It is fundamental to his poetry, increasingly so as his work developed. And yet almost all his poems can be appreciated by people who dismiss his beliefs as wrong-headed. But then, it is possible to read 'The Iliad' without believing that Athene ever existed; just as it is possible to be moved by the visionary poems of Henry Vaughan without believing in any sort of god at all. The universe adumbrated by Yeats deserves respect and does not require belief.

And in the end, the structure is there to sustain the poems. Richard Ellmann, in his biography of the poet, *Yeats, The Man and the Masks,* superseded by later works

in terms of information but not in sympathetic percep-
tiveness, quotes a letter written to Yeats by his father in
1915. It is about Blake, but one feels that J.B. Yeats had
his own son in mind, whether he was giving Willie an
oblique warning or merely trying to explain the process
of poem-making as he saw it:

> 'I know that Blake's poetry is not intelligible without
> a knowledge of Blake's mystical doctrines.
>
> 'Yet mysticism was never the substance of his poetry,
> only its machinery . . . The substance of his poetry
> is himself, revolting and desiring. His mysticism
> was a make-believe, a sort of working hypothesis as
> good as another. He could write about it in prose
> and contentiously assert his belief. When he wrote
> his poems it dropped into the background, and it
> did not matter whether you believed it or not . . .'

The obstinately rationalistic old man would not con-
cede the source of visions and revelations to be more
than 'a working hypothesis', but what he wrote about
'substance' and 'machinery' is as true of W.B. Yeats's work
as it is of all great poetry. Ellmann notes how in 'The
Second Coming' the gyre, such a central item in Yeats's
structure, can be read simply as the spiral of the falcon's
flight, and remain a compelling poetic metaphor, to
someone who has no idea of its wider significance in
what Yeats referred to as *the system*.

CHAPTER NINE

'DECREPIT AGE' AND EXCITED IMAGINATION

In November 1927, concerned again by Yeats's uncertain state of health – he was suffering from congestion of the lungs (he was a cigarette-smoker) and was also in a state of nervous exhaustion – George arranged another long winter holiday. Troubled by poor vision throughout his life, he was by now blind in one eye, and was also beginning to have hearing difficulties. They went to Algeciras in southern Spain, where Morocco, homeland of the original Leo Africanus, was scarcely beyond the horizon. From there they moved to Cannes on the French Riviera, since George wanted him to have expert medical attention, but Yeats was bored and irritated by the prolonged inactivity ordered by the doctor. They moved on into Italy, to Rapallo on the Italian Riviera, where Ezra and Dorothy Pound had made their home. Here, instead of the convalescent or sedentary rich, was an animated youthful group of writers, artists and musicians. Like some great dark-winged swan descending from the north, his arrival even in that turbid pond created excitement among the lesser but gaudy fowl already congregated there. Yeats liked it enormously, and he and George decided to buy a flat there, with the aim of spending their winters in this congenial and stimulating company.

The two Yeats children, Anne and Michael, had been sent to boarding school in Switzerland. There were medical reasons for this. Both had had bouts of illness, and for Michael in particular, mountain air was recommended. At this time tuberculosis, still incurable, was rampant in Ireland and a cause of many child deaths. Nevertheless, the despatch of the children, both under ten, to boarding school also reflects the way in which the household was organized to support their father. Being a family man was important to Yeats in many ways; he was immensely pleased to have children, he enjoyed being able to write 'my bodily heirs'; to know that he too would be an ancestor; but the boisterous and demanding aspects of child-rearing had no charm for him. Apart from looking after Willie, George had his sisters' business in her basement, and was often called to mediate in the battles between the siblings. The Yeatses might perhaps have sent the children to English schools, but that might have been seen as an anti-national gesture: Switzerland was neutral as well as healthy.

On his return to Dublin in spring 1928, he found on his desk a new play for the Abbey, 'The Silver Tassie', submitted by Sean O'Casey. Yeats had lost nothing of his artistic intransigence; he felt the play was not a good one, and refused to produce it. O'Casey, by now an established

Abbey playwright, was dismayed and angry, a flurry of letters ensued; he accused Yeats of having 'hidden shallows', but Yeats was not to be moved. His Irish Literary Theatre would maintain his standards. While he was in Rapallo, his own latest collection of poems had been published in London, to a pleasing reception: critical praise very different to the silence that *A Vision* had toppled into.

The Tower, published 1928, was written between 1919 and 1927. This eight-years' worth of poems spans the time from the end of war to a contentious independence, civil warfare and the uncertain beginnings of a new nation-state, from plain Mr Yeats to Senator-Dr Yeats, Nobel Laureate. It includes the most Christian poem in his canon, 'A Prayer for My Son', shorter and more intense than his poem for Anne, with a sense of *absit omen* in its reference to hostile spirits that might destroy the infant boy, preventing him from growing up to perform a great deed. It makes a direct appeal to an all-powerful god, addressed as You with a capital Y, who once made himself flesh. The poet's precocious feeling of elderliness features in several of these poems, including the title poem, 'The Tower', written in his fiftieth year, where he questions and bemoans:

> '... this absurdity ...
> Decrepit age that has been tied to me
> As to a dog's tail?'

– even though:

> 'Never had I more
> Excited, passionate, fantastical
> Imagination . . .'

– but the musing on age leads quickly into wider themes and deeper thoughts, the age and degeneration of the human world (in his view crumbling at the end of its great gyre) on memories of things past and especially – here he conjures up his own old lusty poet-figure Hanrahan to help him – in a reflective musing on love, the plunge 'Into the labyrinth of another's being'. The third part of the poem, beginning 'It is time that I wrote my will' goes past memory, past the constructs used by the poet in his trade, to the single solitary speaker, declaring his being and his belief, part of which was:

> '. . . being dead, we rise,
> Dream and so create
> Translunar Paradise.'

– his vision of the world beyond was not always paradisal. It was sometimes envisioned by him as a bleak place and by no means a comfortable haven-reward for earthly souls: in 'King and No King', in 1909, he had referred to 'the blinding light beyond the grave' with some foreboding, because of his lack of faith.

A sense of obstinate human dignity is strong in these poems, of the pride and poignant frailty of the lone being, poised against the dissolution of old age; against a country that is breaking apart (as in 'Meditations in Time of Civil War'); against an era of cosmic disintegration:

> 'Another Troy must rise and set,
> Another lineage feed the crow,
> Another Argo's painted prow
> Drive to a flashier bauble yet.'
> ('Two Songs From a Play')

– things that make the poet think of his ancestors and of those who will come after him, who must take up the unrequested gift of life:

> 'Never to have lived is best, ancient writers say. . .
> The second best's a gay goodnight and quickly turn away.'
> (From 'Oedipus at Colonnus')

The collection also contains another of those poems by Yeats which, like 'The Second Coming', is much read in anthologies by those who may not appreciate its context in his thought. 'Leda and the Swan' puts graphic physical sensation into the dry text of a Greek myth in its description of the rape of a girl by Zeus in swan-form. In a typical Yeatsian manner, it ends with a question:

> 'Did she put on his knowledge with his power
> Before the indifferent beak could let her drop?'

– the question which in different forms constantly beset

him. His own knowledge, hard-won, set down with immense pains and thought in *A Vision*, had not gained him power. Perhaps his access to wisdom was incomplete, or even an illusion. Unlike Leda, Yeats had gone out to seek the embrace of the god and never felt it – or hardly ever. But in 1931 he was to write, in the fourth poem of a suite titled *Vacillation,* how when 'my fiftieth year had come and gone', sitting alone in a mundane London coffee shop, he had suddenly felt his body blaze:

> 'And twenty minutes more or less
> It seemed, so great my happiness,
> That I was blessèd and could bless.'

A second term in the Senate would have been possible for Yeats, but his poor health and wish to spend the winter with his young friends at Rapallo made him turn down the chance. His final speech to it had been very brief, and ended by a spasm of intense pain. He had begun his spell in practical politics with enthusiasm, but had come to realize how little could be achieved. The same was true of the great literary and dramatic project. Although the Abbey Theatre was firmly established, its intended function as a beacon of Irish literature and literary integrity was a failure. Other cultural pressures were stronger. Douglas Hyde – to become first President of Ireland in 1938 – though he repudiated the politicizing of his Gaelic League, saw his revival policy become official, with Gaelic a compulsory language in schools. A strong aversion to contemporary literature, music and film arose. Much of what was happening in these areas was regarded as depraved, immoral and anti-religious. Now that political freedom was attained, there was a desire to grow purely Irish flowers in the bowl: simple and plain as they might be, they would not be affected by the rank weeds and poisoned blossoms cultivated elsewhere. In February 1930 an official Censorship Board was set up. All this was detestable to Yeats.

In May 1928, the big house in Merrion Square was sold and they rented a flat in Fitzwilliam Square. Cuala also had to move, and premises were found in Lower Baggot Street. In October the Yeatses moved to Rapallo for the winter. Throughout that year, Yeats had been thinking a great deal about Pound and Pound's work, which found form in *A Packet for Ezra Pound*. Seeing in Pound the same ultimate vision as his own, 'the proclamation of a new divinity', he wanted the wayward, mischief-minded American to emulate his own detachment. Pound's espousal of fascist politics worried him because political involvement pulled in the opposite direction from the pursuit of the divine. The mixture of walks, literary argument and freedom from politics resulted in a burst of creativity in which the poems of *Words for Music Perhaps* were written, eleven of them in two months. The title with its 'experimental' feel harks back to discussions among the Rapallo group of the relations between music and poetry. Another regular member of the Rapallo community was the American musician George Antheil, who would compose scores for Abbey productions of a number of Yeats's works. Most of the poems express the character of 'Crazy Jane', based on a woman Yeats knew of in the old days at Sligo and whom he employs here not at all to portray madness but an elemental sanity that lies at the root of things.

Another arrival in Rapallo was the distinguished German realist playwright Gerhart Hauptmann, who had won the Nobel Prize for Literature in 1912. He was two years older than Yeats, but in better shape; Yeats envied him his ability to drink champagne and take swims in the sea.

In the summer of 1929 the Yeats family removed to the tower at Ballylee. Lady Gregory, now 77, was in declining health, and Yeats, sensitive to the damp from which his western home was not free even in summer, lost much of his enthusiasm for it. In August he became seriously ill, spitting blood and with heavily congested lungs, the physical sickness accompanied by a mental weariness. He was still ill when they left in October for London and then Rapallo. The disease, diagnosed as Malta fever, took the form of a succession of recoveries and relapses – a profoundly depressing syndrome. Yeats wondered if he was the victim of a malevolent spell. On Christmas Eve 1929 he made his will, witnessed by Pound and Pound's disciple the young northern English poet Basil Bunting: he left everything he possessed to George to be used for the children's benefit.

He expected to die, but recovered slowly. He grew a

beard for the second time in his life. Madame Blavatsky had persuaded him to remove his black beard; this
was white, and its removal symbolized the end of his
illness. It was already July of 1930 when he returned
to Ireland, spending some recuperative time at Coole
before taking up residence in Fitzwilliam Square. He
was pleased around this time to discover the work of a
new generation of young Irish writers, among them Liam
O'Flaherty, Sean O'Faolain, and Frank O'Connor; their
realism was not his own form, but he perceived both
talent and artistic integrity.

In summer 1931 Yeats went to England. He was to re-
ceive an honorary doctorate from Oxford University and
he was also involved in the publication of a complete 'Edition de luxe' of his works. At a lunch given in his honour
in London he met an Indian teacher, Shri Purohit Swami,
a Hindu wise man. Yeats took to him immediately. He
shared two qualities of the poet's own, a certain stately
courtliness and formality of manner, and a simple and
spontaneous soul within, capable of great perception. Impressed by the remarks and conversation of the Swami,
Yeats urged him to write a spiritual autobiography, which
the Swami proceeded to do, with great success. Yeats
wrote an introduction. In the winter of 1931–32, the
Yeatses did not return to Rapallo; he was too concerned
about Lady Gregory, and was spending most of his time
at Coole. George remained at home. Being Mrs Yeats
meant a large amount of work. She dealt not only with
every household matter, and the Abbey, but also with the

extensive non-personal correspondence of her husband, and as his editor-researcher. At this time too, Cuala was again struggling, and Lily's embroidery department had to be closed down as its turnover and profits could not sustain its employees.

On the night of April 28, 1932, Lady Gregory died. Yeats, who had come briefly back to Dublin on theatre business, received the message of her imminent death too late to be with her as he had wished. He felt bereft. Augusta Gregory had been friend, patron, collaborator, and more than all that: 'mother, friend, sister and brother'. He was weeping as Lady Gregory's granddaughter came to pick him up at the railway station. Coole was no longer to be a haven; the great house was speedily stripped of its furnishings. Robert Gregory's widow, a brisk Welshwoman, had no interest in the big, remote house; she would bring up her children elsewhere. Coole had already been sold to the Forestry Department of the state, and was being rented back by Lady Gregory. As if to compensate, George found the family a country house, Riversdale, at Rathfarnham, just south of Dublin, with spacious grounds. But Yeats felt the loss of his friend profoundly. He recorded later that following her death: 'I found I had written no verse for two years; I had never been so long barren'; and speculated: 'Perhaps Coole Park where I had escaped from politics, from all that Dublin talked of, when it was shut, shut me out from my theme; or did the subconscious drama that was my imaginative life end with its owner?'

The election of 1932 saw the defeat of Cosgrave's government and the formation of a Fianna Fail government under de Valera. The change of government was accomplished democratically, but there was accompanying violence. General O'Duffy, chief of the Garda Siochana under Cosgrave, was sacked by de Valera and became head of the Army Comrades' Association, soon to be known as the Blueshirts, and set up in open emulation of Mussolini and his Blackshirts.

Yeats was sufficiently recovered to withstand the rigours of an American lecture tour, and spent October to December travelling in the USA. He was raising money partly on his own account but partly also for a new project of his, the Irish Academy of Letters, which had been launched in September. As time had gone on, winnowing both lives and reputations, Yeats himself and George Bernard Shaw had emerged as the two titans of Irish literature (Joyce, who took no part in Irish affairs, was a ghost-third; Beckett was still unknown). The Academy was the brain-child of Yeats and Shaw, who saw it both as a necessary institution for the independent state with its own cultural path to chart; and very much also as a stronghold of the principles of free expression:

'There is in Ireland an official censorship possessing, actively exercising, powers of suppression.'

– Irish writers could be published in the United States or Britain, and be banned in their own country. The

Abbey Theatre, which received a useful state subsidy of
£1,000, received a letter from the Ministry of Finance
to warn it that future subsidies would be conditional on
the theatre's repertoire being acceptable. This brought a
stern and uncompromising reply from Yeats, not merely
rejecting the warning, but refusing any further aid from
the government: as long as the Abbey existed, it would
retain its freedom. There was an inconclusive meeting
between the Taoiseach and the poet, and the government
eventually dropped the threat in 1933.

This was the year in which the Falange was founded
in Spain; the year in which Hitler became Chancellor
of Germany. Ireland was suffering in the international
economic disaster of the Great Depression. The capi-
talist economies seemed to be played out, with no-one
knowing how to take a grip on things. Yeats had already
diagnosed the problem on a universal scale. He was
seeing on the earthly plane the consequences of the
gathering dissolution as the cosmic gyre of Objectivity
lost energy to the countervailing one of Subjectivity. He
had no belief in the collective wisdom of the people; had
never been impressed by what had happened in Russia
since 1917, seeing in that another manifestation of collapse. His anti-democratic stance led him into a brief
and embarrassing flirtation with General O'Duffy's
Blueshirts, a Fascist-style movement which for a moment
seemed to be a force in Irish politics until de Valera successfully outfaced O'Duffy in August. Yeats wrote some
songs for the Blueshirts which, politics quite apart, rank

as the nadir of his poetic output in their hollowness and lack of conviction. He was not tempted into further support, and the common sense of George, who loathed the Fascists, may have helped to keep his enthusiasm within bounds.

In that year he published a new collection of poems, *The Winding Stair*. The title in this case is not shared with one of the poems, but affirms a continuation of themes with *The Tower;* Yeats had already developed the image of the stairway of Thoor Ballylee as a metaphor, and in 'Blood and the Moon' spells it out: 'This winding, gyring, spiring treadmill of a stair is my ancestral stair' – but the ancestors are not Pollexfens and Yeatses, they are Goldsmith, Swift, Berkeley, Burke – intellectual and tutelary ancestors; in the case of the last three bound up very much with his current reading and thinking, philosophical and political.

There is much irony in this collection, and a profusion of sharp, epigrammatic one- or two-line phrases; also a number of suggestive short poems, incorporating incidental insights, like 'The Nineteenth Century and After', which makes a riposte to the depression of Matthew Arnold's 'Dover Beach'. These poems and their predecessors owe much to the intensive reading he had been doing in order to revise *A Vision,* writing in its revised introduction: 'I put *The Tower* and *The Winding Stair* into evidence to show my poetry has gained in self-possession and power.'

By now Yeats is the accomplished master of technique

and the fashioning of rhythm and structure to be at one with thought. The range goes without apparent effort from the light, teasingly admiring tone of 'For Anne Gregory' to the incantatory lines, the daring imagery, the unearthly resonances, of 'Byzantium'. His old, great love could still stir his muse. 'Quarrel in Old Age' was prompted by a dispute with Maud Gonne over the treatment of women hunger-strikers; its cross tone still melts into the memory of a far-off spring.

Yeats was now approaching the age of seventy. He had been ill, he had almost died, he felt in some ways decrepit. Not least, he was feeling some anxiety about his sexual capacity. He felt that his libido was weakening. For a poet who saw in sexual ecstasy one of the portals of insight, and who knew that sexual desire had transformed, and informed, his verse, this was an aspect of ageing perhaps more alarming than other debilities. He knew of the rejuvenatory fame of the 'monkey gland' operation developed by the German doctor Steinach.

In 1934 he travelled to London in order to have the operation, performed by the Harley Street doctor Norman Haire. Haire was by no means a typical medical consultant. A bluff, coarsely spoken Australian, with non-establishment opinions on many subjects from sexual freedom to hygienic clothing to the desirability of 'racial purity'.

Yeats's treatment, which included a form of vasectomy, had a remarkable effect. Whether it was all in the mind, or whether it did have a rejuvenating effect on his body, he felt stronger and more vigorous in every way (among the cynical literati of Dublin's pubs he acquired a new nickname, 'the Gland Old Man').

The poems of 1934 are troubled, prompted by political fears and anger ('Parnell's Funeral'), personal doubts:

> 'God guard me from the thoughts men think
> In the mind alone . . .'

– he wanted to end his days a passionate man, if seen also as a foolish one; and engaged himself in a vehement, part-philosophical, part-intuitive verbal wrestling with the sources of creation. For these he personifies the struggle in the person of Ribh, an Irish hermit and heretical monk who has trained himself to think the unthinkable. The imagery of the twelve Supernatural Songs is bold and fierce, concerned with the spasms of creation, struggling to encompass the concept of self-regeneration as the divine quality, far superior to the 'copying' of earthly reproduction. For Ribh, divinity – godhead – is an endless act of self-engendering: 'Eternity is passion'.

Even for one who believed ardently in the notion of general renewal, of self-renewal, and of accepting the guidance of unseen powers, Yeats's last five years form perhaps the most remarkable phase of his life. By seventy, many men come round to a mood of regret for a misspent youth. Yeats was no exception, but his regret was for his long, solitary, onanistic years which he now saw as a sterile period, and wished that he had been earlier

released into sexual fulfilment and freedom. The theories
of Haire, the promiscuity of Pound, his worldly awareness of the semi-secret or open infidelities of so many of
his friends and acquaintances, all spurred him on. The
evolution of his relationship with his wife into one in
which she was much more his housekeeper, comforter,
medicine-bottle minder, business manager and mother to
his children, rather than any longer a partner in the passionate adventures either of the bed or the spirit-séance,
enabled him to conduct affairs with an openness to which
she displayed remarkable forbearance. Sean O'Faolain,
who became a friend of Yeats at this time, went so far –
too far, surely – as to later describe George as acting as
the old man's 'procuress'.

In June 1934, the Yeatses gave up their flat in Rapallo,
which was taken over by Ezra Pound's parents. In the
Italian resort to collect their possessions, Yeats showed
Pound the mauscript of a play he had just completed,
'The King of the Great Clock Tower'. Pound's reply was
swift and damning: 'Putrid'. He thought Yeats was played
out. After this episode, the two poets would go their different ways, though Yeats was pleased to find Pound had
a better opinion of his later poems, in 1938. Yeats was an
honoured attender at a conference in Rome later that
year, where he spoke on 'Dramatic Theatre' to an audience that included Pirandello and Maeterlinck. London
and southern England once again became the focus of his
life. He had earlier met, and almost immediately begun
an affair with a young actress, Margaret Ruddock, whose

stage name was Margot Collis. Unstable and depressive, Margot was also a writer of poems. Yeats saw an 'intellectual passion' in her, and for the first time ever, wrote a poem to a named woman, Margot, hymning the renewal, through her, of the Age of Miracles.

Olivia Shakespear was his confidante in this escapade. She asked him, perceptively, 'don't you feel rather as though you had been wound up again?' The poet, who referred to Haire's operation on him as having given him a 'strange second puberty' went on to establish a simultaneous liaison with an attractive young Anglo-Irishwoman, Ethel Mannin. In her mid-thirties, she was already a successful writer, a believer in sexual freedom and keenly left-wing in politics. She had written 'sex is life, and all art sexual.' Yeats was entranced, but did not know that Norman Haire had encouraged Ethel to assess his post-operative sexual performance. At this time he was attending Haire's clinic on a daily basis for further 'monkey gland' treatment.

It was his lungs that let him down, however. He returned home in January 1935 for George's care, writing frequent letters to Margot and Ethel, and reading *The Arabian Nights* until George took it away as too stimulating. As soon as his health let him, he returned to London, still hungry for adventure. He had also accepted the commission to compile the *Oxford Book of Modern Verse*. A long-time friend, Lady Ottoline Morrell, introduced him to Lady Dorothy Wellesley in May 1935; she was the estranged wife of a son of the Duke of Wellington. Dorothy Wellesley was bisexual and had affairs with both men and women. In Yeats, her mannishness brought out what he called his feminine strain. Lady Dorothy's lesbian partner lived in a house in the grounds of her stately home, Penns in the Rocks, in Sussex. It was a very different kind of household from Coole in every way except that it occupied the same upper-class society bracket and attendant comforts. He became a regular guest at Penns, with his own room, and found it a place which inspired him to write and work.

Yeats's brief to compile what would be the authoritative guide to modern English poetry was a challenging one for him and he gave it much thought. It also placed him in a position where he could make someone's reputation overnight. This was not lost upon Margot Ruddock. Yeats, while sympathetic to new poets and new talent, found it difficult to appreciate the work of such poets as W.H. Auden and T.S. Eliot. He did not care for political verse, and to him, who had striven so hard to absorb, distil and recreate his own influences, the eclectic allusiveness of Eliot seemed hardly proper poetry at all.

In 1935 his friend George Russell, 'AE', died, and Yeats was unimpressed by the grand public funeral which followed. For his own seventieth birthday he was given a gift which, like Sato's sword years before, both gave him an image and concentrated his mind. It was a Chinese carving in lapis lazuli, showing two figures in a landscape with a mountain, temple and trees. Yeats saw them as a

teacher and his pupil, and it brought back his old interest
in the east. The giver, Harry Clifton, would be finely
repaid in the poem dedicated to him, 'Lapis Lazuli'. That
year Yeats turned down an invitation to be Professor of
Poetry at Harvard and arranged to spend the winter in
Majorca, with Shri Purohit Swami, where they would
work together translating the Sanskrit *Upanishads* into
English. Of the party would be the Swami's follower and
patron, Mrs Gwyneth Foden. George Yeats remained at
Rathfarnham.

   Yeats did not judge the Swami harshly. He knew that
he relied chiefly on rich women for support, though he
was not above touching Yeats himself for a loan. Mrs
Foden had been the Swami's mistress, and attempted to
combine the roles of tour manager, matron and spiritual
handmaiden. Neither Yeats nor Shri Purohit took her
seriously; the poet and the Indian sage worked on together; in the mornings the poet worked on his own
new project, *The Herne's Egg*; later in the day was time
for the collaboration. Then in January 1936 Yeats fell ill
again. A local doctor diagnosed both heart disease and
kidney trouble, nephritis. George was sent for and flew,
literally, to his side, arriving by air, the children following
later. On George's arrival, Mrs Foden abruptly departed
for London. Yeats's return to health was gradual, and she
had to nurse him for more than two months. He was
scarcely recovered when they were visited by a distraught
and clearly not quite sane Margot Ruddock. Until
George's arrival Yeats had been corresponding regularly

with her, and others; critical remarks made by him about her new poems had worked on her already unbalanced mind until she finally made her way to Majorca after him, to find, instead of her attentive London lover, an elderly invalid with a formidable wife and two teenage children. The Swami, to whom she had given money, now returned her some. Apparently somewhat soothed, she left the island for Barcelona, but there she jumped out of a window and was taken to hospital. Yeats and George travelled to Barcelona to see to her safe return to London. But the story was a rich one for rumour-mongers. Out of loyalty to Margot, or belief in her poetic talent, he did not drop his support for her work. He did not consider madness a bar to poetry, indeed quite the reverse, as did A.E. Housman in a famous lecture, *The Name and Nature of Poetry,* published in 1935. But he did not see Margot again for some time, and then it was to discuss her reading of some of his poems on the BBC; the affair was over. Her mental disorders continued, and she was eventually committed to an asylum where she remained an inmate until her death in 1951.

Majorca already had its resident English-language poets in Robert Graves and Laura Riding, whose menage was also not without its sudden exits through upper-storey windows. But Graves and Yeats did not establish friendly relations; though Yeats wished to include both him and Riding in his Oxford anthology, they were angered by his rejection of their protegé James Reeves, and refused to be included. They were wise; when

the anthology was published, its selection was widely
criticized. Yeats gave Margot Ruddock equal promi-
nence with T.S. Eliot. He included only three poems
by W.H. Auden, who at that stage was by no means a
newcomer to the scene. Dorothy Wellesley had eight
poems, her friend W.J. Turner had twelve. Yeats had
failed to be Olympian; he had failed to apprehend or
sympathize with the course modern English poetry was
taking; he had played favourites. But those who saw
the book as the personal choice of a great poet were
pleased enough; its long Introduction remains a useful
key to Yeats's thoughts on poetry; and its sales pleased
both the publisher and the compiler.

In the summer of 1936, the Swami returned to
India, George returned to Ireland, and Yeats, well
again, returned to London, or rather to Penns in the
Rocks. His relationship with Dorothy Wellesley had
reached a new intensity. Despite her lesbianism, she
felt a powerful attraction to Yeats, and she and he began
to exchange versions of a long, mildly pornographic
ballad-type poem, whose theme is love at second-
hand. Its theme, familiar from stage farce, is that of a
noblewoman who had her maid act as a substitute lover
for her, under cover of darkness. Between Yeats and
Dorothy Wellesley, it became a sexual game in which
they could share excitements, switch genders, indulge
fantasies, without physical connection. Thus revived,
he returned to home and family after a long stay. But,
later that year, he returned to Penns. He had been

invited to deliver the BBC's annual National Lecture, on modern poetry. George Yeats provided Dorothy with a list of his dietary and medical requirements, and gave instructions about when he should rest. She had had enough of emergency dashes to his bedside, and told Dorothy she thought this would be his last solo visit to England. There were delicious interludes with his hostess before and after his delivery of the lecture. He wrote to her afterwards of:

> '. . . that spectacle of personified sunlight. I can never while I live forget your movement across the room just before I left, the movement made to draw attention to the boy in yourself.'

With Dorothy Wellesley, Yeats was safe in a literary-sexual never-never land in which she was a lithe boy and he could imagine himself 'a girl of nineteen for certain hours'. Ethel Mannin sought to drag him into the real life of the 1930s, as the Nazi government intensified its hold on the German people and the concentration camps began to fill. Yeats, who had accepted the Goethe Prize in 1934 from the Nazi-dominated city of Frankfurt, refused to be dragged. Asked by Mannin to lend his weight to the campaign to have the 1936 Nobel Peace Prize awarded to the imprisoned German pacifist poet Karl von Ossietsky, he made a somewhat embarrassed refusal. Critical spirits have seen in this further evidence of Yeats's continuing sympathy with the European dic-

tators at a time when even those who had formerly
been seduced were beginning to see the reality. But his
position was not inconsistent. In the middle of the First
World War he had declared that war was not a poet's
business. He told his friend that he had no interest in
politics outside those of Ireland, and Ireland was far from
the European mainstream. He was at pains to deny that
he was uncaring: 'I am not callous, every nerve trembles
with horror at what is happening in Europe.'

He asked Ethel Mannin to read 'The Second Coming', to understand how he had foreseen the approach
of evil days. Although he was concerned to maintain
her affection and good opinion, there is no reason to
doubt his overall sincerity. She challenged him again,
when he wrote a poem in vindication of Roger Casement, to ask him why he still took a pension from the
British government. Again he had to resort to lengthy
self-justification:

> 'It was given at a time when Ireland was represented
> in Parliament and voted out of the taxes of both
> countries . . . it was explained to me that it implied
> no political bargain . . .'

Ethel, whom he described to Dorothy in distant
terms as an 'extreme revolutionist' of his acquaintance,
was important to him. In a sense, she replaced Maud
Gonne, who decades earlier had nagged Yeats about his
Laodicean politics and lack of involvement. Yeats, who

knew that he had not many years to live, was reliving aspects of his life. (James Stephens, a fellow-mystic, was to write of Yeats: 'he died in a spring-time, and younger than when he was born'.) His chosen women reflected his needs and his drives. He was experiencing a fulfilment that his long-drawn-out youth and literary apprenticeship had not known. Lady Gregory was dead, but there was Lady Dorothy. Maud was a distant figure now, but there was Ethel. And there was George, the home, the anchor, the family, writing matter-of-factly to his other women to remind them of his medications. But the tale of the old man's younger lovers was not yet complete.

CHAPTER TEN

'WHEN AN OLD MAN'S BLOOD GROWS COLD'

At the start of 1937, Yeats felt sufficiently vigorous to consider a voyage to India, where he would rejoin the Swami. But the promise of Indian asceticism finally did not lure him. The prospect of even weeks of sexual abstinence now alarmed him: 'I believe that if I repressed this for any long period I would break down under the strain as did the great Ruskin' he wrote to the Swami. He was ripe for romance. In April, his friend Edmund Dulac introduced him to a celebrated journalist, Edith Shackleton Heald, who lived with her sister in a fine house in the West Sussex village of Steyning. She was a forceful, witty asserter of women's rights, but Yeats, whose 'Prayer for My Daughter', and subsequent casual attitude to his daughter's education, were ample evidence of his lack of concern on this subject (something he shared with his political opponent de Valera and most other Irishmen of his time) found she had many other interests. They had met on odd occasions before, and she had noted his 'grave manners and melodious conversation'. Now they fell in love. His plans to go back to Rathfarnham were postponed for a time, and when he did go home, he wrote her letters full of hope for their relationship: 'a friendship from which I hope so much. You seem to have that kind of understanding or sympathy which is peace.' Back in London, based in a little flat which Dulac found for him at 52 Holland Park, he and she consummated their affair. Edith, aged fifty-three, retained a youthful figure. She was petite compared to him, her head scarcely reaching past his shoulder; but they made a handsome couple. Despite a tendency to be overweight, he never became obese. Edith, though she appears to have had no qualms about a physical relationship with Yeats, was another woman of ambiguous sexuality. After Yeats's death she would adopt an openly lesbian lifestyle. Yeats throughout his life showed a public, as well as a private, support for sexual liberty, from his support for Wilde to his lack of concern about whether Casement was a homosexual or not. In these times, in a man who alters his wife's name to George, who gravitates in his love affairs towards lesbian women, one might seek to detect signs of a sexual ambivalence.

In letters, Yeats spoke frankly of his feminine compo-nent. In daily life, he could exhibit a remarkable pas-sivity. He relied upon George to organize him much of the time, though as he became more dependent, he rebelled against it, seeing it as a loss of freedom rather than a choice. Sado-masochistic activity of a mild sort had an appeal for him: the application of taws to bottom recurs in his poems, and on one occasion, in 'The Poem

of Lancelot Switchback', of 1937, written for Dorothy
Wellesley, becomes explicit:

> 'A beating on the buttocks
>   Will warm your heart and mine.'

– underlying all this was the late developer's sense of
sexual inadequacy, the crushing weight of Maud Gonne's
rejections, and the old man's fear of impotence.

Many years before, in the early stages of their married
life, the 'automatic writing' had been in part a regulator
of sexual behaviour for the Yeatses, enabling George,
always referred to in the third person as 'the medium', to
take account of his failures and fatigues in a tactful way,
while also providing for the conjugal intimacies that she
herself very much desired as well as seeing in them the
necessary basis of a successful and productive marriage.

Now Yeats hymned himself as a 'wild old wicked
man'. One writer on his life, David Pierce in *Yeats's
Worlds* (1995) echoes another, John Harwood, in *Olivia
Shakespear and W.B. Yeats* (1989) is saying that this was a
mask: 'by the mid-1930s Yeats was suffering from high
blood pressure, heart disease, kidney disease, rheuma-
tism, poor circulation and chronic respiratory infec-
tions. Even climbing stairs proved difficult.' This is to
miss the point. For Yeats, whose inner life was as intense
as it ever had been, seething in its realization of time
running out and things yet undone, it was the defective,
lumbering crock of a body that masked the truth. When

the body finally seized up, the spirit would remain. Yeats
was concerned to get his spirit into the right state before
its transference to another mode of being. He believed
that a spirit which had not accomplished its earthly
function would remain tied to the earth, a pathetic,
ghost-like entity, unable to soar into the cosmos. In a
real sense, he was working to ensure that his own future
state would be untrammelled in this way. That is not
to say he was not enjoying himself, nor that his emo-
tions were unspontaneous. Among the feelings in his
late poems is a sense of relief. 'The Gyres', written in
1936–37, turns its back on the hermit-voices of earlier
poets whose cave-voices echoed: 'Repent!'–

> '. . . Out of Cavern comes a voice
> And all it knows is that one word "Rejoice".'

– in the poem which follows it, 'Lapis Lazuli' -

> 'All things fall and are built again
> And those that build them again are gay.'

– his joy was genuine but enriched by a sense of gratitude and fulfilled purpose. For a man who still retained
his fascination with matters occult ('Sex, Philosophy and
the Occult preoccupy him' wrote Dorothy Wellesley in
October 1937), the liaisons and the poems of his later
years would have appeared not as a freak, or a happy
chance, but as something due and long-charted in the

slow progression of the stars, and a further justification to his belief that his long struggle to come to terms with the spirit world had been worthwhile.

In August 1937, Yeats made a speech at a banquet given by the Irish Academy of Letters to two Irish Americans who had come from the Testimonial Committee for W.B. Yeats, to present him with $6,000 as a tribute to his achievement for Ireland. This was gratifying to the poet who felt strongly that the narrow Catholic orthodoxy newly enshrined in the national constitution was a bad thing for the country; and who knew that to many Catholics, he was not a national treasure, but a man of sin and an evil influence on the nation. His speech made reference to the long struggle, begun when Lady Gregory was still alive, to secure the Hugh Lane pictures for the National Gallery in Dublin. A poem about the Gallery had been forming in his mind, and he promised to send a copy of it to all the 500 prominent Irish-Americans who had contributed to his Testimonial. In the following month, 'The Municipal Gallery Revisited' was completed and duly despatched. Other business in Ireland also claimed his attention. The Cuala Press, which had always led a hand-to-mouth existence, and on which he had spent a lot of money, was heavily in debt and under threat of closure. Fierce arguments with Lolly took place. While Lily, who ran the embroidery side, was content to work to Willie's diktat, Lolly resented his interference and felt that his attitude, as editorial director of the press, had prevented it from growing; and that he grumbled at the business's financial state without troubling to read or understand the accounts which she regularly sent him. She was only three years younger than he but there was no suggestion that she would retire from the business, which could scarcely support a professional manager. In the event George Yeats was to run Cuala for some years after Lolly's death.

The Cuala Press had been engaged in producing a series of 'Broadsheets', attractively printed works of Irish authors, illustrated by Jack Yeats. Now W.B. Yeats contributed a further short work, *On the Boiler*, published in October 1938. Loosely modelled on John Ruskin's *Fors Clavigera,* it is in part an intemperate response to the new Irish constitution, proclaiming a republic. The man who had written in a marching song for O'Duffy: 'What's equality? Muck in the yard', still places his hope in great men:

> 'Think first how many able men the country has . . . and mould your system upon those men. It does not matter how you get them, but get them. Republics, Kingdoms, Soviets, Corporate States, Parliaments, are trash, as Hugo said of something else "not worth one blade of grass that God gives for the nest of the linnet".'

Associated with this was Yeats's expressed belief that: 'Since about 1900 the better stocks have not been replacing their numbers, while the stupider and less healthy have been more than replacing theirs.' He was deliberately trailing his coat, but the shallow thinking, the purblind snobbery of such notions as that people living on inherited incomes are more intelligent than those who work for their living, are indefensible. The title of the tract is taken from his recollection of a half-mad ship's carpenter in Sligo, who used to climb on to an old rusty boiler to declaim his thoughts. It is the only hint of self-irony in the work.

While writing it, he was agitating about going to Monte Carlo with Edith Shackleton. As agreed with George, he would go with Edith and they would stay there together; then she would come later, 'taking over' from Edith. While there, he worked on correcting the proofs of *New Poems,* covering work between 1936 and late 1937. For a month he and Edith were together. After George had arrived to take over — as in a military handover, one woman departed as the next arrived — he wrote love letters to Edith, wishing she were still with him, and full of anticipation of the poems he was going to write. The efficient George had found a new hotel, the Idéal-Séjour, at Cap-Martin, looking out to sea, with a garden and good food.

Dorothy Wellesley who, like Margot Ruddock, was a poet of talent, was also subject to fits of depression, and drank heavily when she felt things were going badly. Since the arrival of Edith in Yeats's life, the erotic relationship with Dorothy had cooled off — and he now had a room of his own in the comfortable Shackleton

Heald house – but the friendship and attraction of Penns remained. He gave constructive criticism of her poetry and valuable moral encouragement. On their return from the Cote d'Azur, he spent a week at Penns and then six weeks at Steyning. Back in Ireland his son had chickenpox, his daughter was being fractious – but George was coping. Yeats was free to write poems, and he also wrote the powerful, bleak short play 'Purgatory', which was included with *On the Boiler* as a dramatic rendering of the author's ideas. Set against the background of a burnt-out mansion in post-Ascendancy Ireland but rich in resonances that reach back into the Greek myths, its central character is an 'Old Man' who has killed his father and in the course of the action kills his only son. The fact that his mother died in giving him birth completes his circle of guilt.

George was more sympathetic to Edith Shackleton Heald than to Dorothy Wellesley because Yeats could write more easily in Edith's company; she was a support rather than a drain on his energy and emotional vitality. In a letter to Edith, she acknowledged the mental stimulus, and mourned 'And nobody can feel more passionately than I do that he has to return to this desolate place.' The desolation was an emotional one. Yeats's return to Rathfarnham in the rainy summer of 1938 was a brief one before he went back to Steyning and Penns, but mostly Steyning.

The *New Poems* of 1938, a substantial and varied collection of thirty-four poems, show the different facets of the

post-operative Yeats. The contorted, visceral brooding of
the 1934 poems is largely gone. Many of these are public
poems, focused outwards, addressed to an individual or
an imagined public. 'Parnell's Funeral' (1934) had been
full of cannibalistic imagery, harsh scorn and bitterness:

> 'All that was said in Ireland is a lie . . .
> Saving the rhyme rats hear before they die.'

– 'Come Gather Round Me Parnellites' (September
1936) is far lighter in tone, with an ironic glint rather
than a contemptuous lash. The poet has achieved some
political detachment, and wrote around this time to
Ethel Mannin: 'I am finished with that forever.' It was
as a patriot, not a party man, that he wrote 'Roger Casement' and 'The Ghost of Roger Casement', at a time
when it appeared that Casement's homosexual diaries
had been forged by the British, and 'Roger Casement'
was published in de Valera's government organ, the *Irish
Press*. His new woman friends provide themes, Margot
Ruddock in 'A Crazed Girl', Dorothy Wellesley in 'To
a Friend', in which he wishes his fellow-poet the peril-
ous joys of inspiration, on her stair: 'The Proud Furies
each with torch held high.' His own state of physical
and mental release is defiantly proclaimed in 'The Spur':

> 'You think it horrible that lust and rage
> Should dance attendance on my old age;
> They were not such a plague when I was young;

What else have I to spur me into song?'

– this was written to Dorothy Wellesley, his collaborator in sexy balladry, who however felt that Yeats had gone too far, in public anyway, with the two 'Chambermaid's Songs' of impotence, also included in *New Poems*. Two fine, stately poems of recollection, 'Beautiful Lofty Things' and 'The Municipal Gallery Revisited', pay tribute to those dead or in his past. In the first, he recalled his father, facing the Abbey mob; 'his beautiful mischievous head thrown back'; in the second John Synge, 'that rooted man'; in both Augusta Gregory, her courage, her breeding – the second poem of the two ending with the often-quoted lines:

'Think where man's glory most begins and ends
And say my glory was I had such friends.'

Sincere as the tribute was, Yeats knew well where his true glory lay, but he also knew what he owed. None of these were in themselves new themes. What is new in the *New Poems* is the note of joviality. The old man who has seen and thought so much, whose battered but intact sensibility has endured so much, can now look back and forward and laugh, in a way that would certainly have shocked the aesthetic and serious W.B. Yeats of the 1890s. But the laughter incorporates that younger Yeats and his ideas, it is a complex emotion that blends tragedy and joy. Yeats himself had used the phrase 'tragic joy' (line 8 of 'The Gyres') as early as 1904 in a piece he wrote for Samhain, and the state is summed up in one of his last poems, 'Under Ben Bulben':

> 'Know that when all words are said
> And a man is fighting mad,
> Something drops from eyes long blind,
> He completes his partial mind,
> For an instant stands at ease,
> Laughs aloud, his heart at peace.'

Fused together at the core of the moment of ultimate exhilaration are a number of complex elements. Tragic joy arises out of dissolution: the joy of the breaking-up of things, the joy of anticipation of a new order, the joy achieved in self-fulfilment when every faculty of our being is engaged and unaware of itself; the joy of being at one with the whole vast universe of spirit; a hint of the blessed states that lie beyond life; and the rapture of the artist in forming all this into his creation in a way that could not be improved on.

This concentration of feeling is what gives such poems as 'The Gyres' and 'Lapis Lazuli' their distinctive character. They look upon destruction, even destruction of the beautiful:

> 'No handiwork of Callimachus
> Who handled marble as if it were bronze,
> Made draperies that seemed to rise
> When sea-wind swept the corner, stands.'

– not to mourn, or shrug, or pontificate, but, in 'The Gyres', to laugh, for to be smashed and remade is the order of things; and, in 'Lapis Lazuli', for the same reason, even in the inscrutable old Chinese faces:

> 'Their eyes, mid many wrinkles, their eyes,
> Their ancient glittering eyes, are gay.'

In the whirlwind year of 1938, Yeats, as he raced towards his death, would not sustain the mood of laughter and the expression of tragic joy. But these poems of 1936 and 1937 remain his most finished response to the problematic nature of the individual earthbound being within the great metaphysical system he himself had delineated.

The production of 'Purgatory' by the Abbey, in August 1938, was in part a father-daughter collaboration; the stage design was by the nineteen-year old Anne Yeats. It was a critical success. Its source in Yeats's eugenic beliefs (the aristocratic mother had made the genetic error of falling in love with and marrying the loutish stable-boy) was submerged in the stark power of the verse and the dramatic setting.

Anne Yeats's arrival as a set-designer for the Abbey was more the result of her own persistence than the prompting and support of her father. He saw his paternal role in grandly dynastic terms rather than in any practical details of helping his children. He was a remote father, even when he was resident in the household. Even to Michael he did not talk a great deal. There was no repetition, for his son, of the expansive breakfast sessions he himself as a teenager had had with J.B. Yeats. As the children grew older, the relationship grew easier. They could play him (and he could be beaten) at croquet and chess, but Yeats was closer and more affectionate to his daughter than to his son.

He had not seen Maud Gonne for a long time, though they had exchanged infrequent letters. Now she came to tea at Riversdale. After so many poems in which her identity could only be inferred, he had in 1937 named her, in 'Beautiful Lofty Things', along with others whom he recalled in splendid moments; hers was a snapshot view:

'Maud Gonne at Howth station waiting a train,
Pallas Athene in that straight back and arrogant head ...'

Now Maud was an old woman. The implacable beautiful face with its broad cheeks had crumpled and wrinkled but her eyes were still sternly idealistic. They talked about dreams of long ago, and Yeats was roused to enthusiasm. As she left, he said: 'Maud, we should have gone on with our Castle of the Heroes, we might still do it.' Maud was about to publish her autobiography, *A Servant of the Queen,* a work which Yeats thoroughly disliked. She outlived him by fourteen years, dying at the age of eighty-seven in 1953.

When he was away from Edith Shackleton Heald, he wrote her yearning letters, signed W.B. Yeats. Throughout his adult life he had disliked his first name, especially in the form used by his family and closest friends, Willie or Willy; he had asked new lovers not to use it. He was hoping for another winter like the previous one, with Edith, at the Hotel Idéal-Séjour. In the meantime he was arranging for his own burial and epitaph. His procedure recalls that of his grandfather, the formidable George Pollexfen, who would call daily at the Anglican church in Sligo to check on the progress of his tomb. The poems of summer and autumn 1938 are written in a clear-eyed, if not serene, anticipation of death. He was not reticent about this, sending a draft of 'Under Ben Bulben' to Ethel Mannin for her comments ('I like your epitaph', she said). He had chosen the place where he wanted to be buried, at Drumcliffe in County Sligo; and written the epitaph of which Mannin approved. His sister Lily was less enthusiastic, writing to him to say that the Yeats family did not go in for tombstones: 'The family has always been very gay.'

In recent years, Olivia Shakespear had become more peripheral to his life, but her death in October 1938 shocked him. He was ill himself, with lumbago, and his thoughts turned to his first meetings with her, and to the place she had occupied in his life for so long: 'For more than forty years she has been the centre of my life in London'; he could not now bear the thought of London without her.

By this time, most of Yeats's English friends had come to realize that a war with Hitler's Germany was going to happen. Dorothy Wellesley warned Yeats of the danger of being trapped abroad, if hostilities broke out suddenly. Yeats, most unwilling to give up the thought of the winter excursion to Cap Martin, put his faith in the Munich Agreement between Hitler and the British Prime Minister Chamberlain, who returned to London to utter the later-notorious promise, 'Peace in our time'. Sustained by Edith, he was still busy writing, and completed his last play, 'The Death of Cuchulain', by the end of November, when George arrived to travel south with him.

A congenial group of friends and acquaintances were also wintering in the area. Ten miles away at Beaulieu were Lady Dorothy Wellesley and her lover Hilda Matthews; also nearby were Dermod O'Brien, President of the Royal Hibernian Academy of Arts, and his wife. Edith Shackleton Heald, whom Yeats would have most liked to be of the company, was not due to arrive until late January, when she would take over the caring role from George Yeats.

Like heirs beginning to argue over the family heirlooms before the death, Dorothy and Edith, both strong and possessive women, were at odds over Yeats, each convinced that he was 'hers', rather than the other's. Anticipating her arrival with increasing excitement, Yeats wrote to Edith that he felt better than he had for years. At the same time he was writing to another woman friend, Lady Elizabeth Pelham, with whom his relationship was intellectual and spiritual (she was a mystic and occultist) that he knew his time would not be long. In his penultimate poem, 'Cuchulain Comforted', he wrote of the strange phase after death, when:

'A man that had six mortal wounds, a man
Violent and famous, strode among the dead.'

– to find himself in no hall of heroes but among twittering shades, 'Convicted cowards all by kindred slain.'

On the 21st of January 1939, he wrote what was to be his last poem, 'The Black Tower'. A wind of eternity blows through the lines of this poem, which tells of the soldiers who still stand guard in the tower of a dead or forgotten king:

'There in the tomb the dark grows blacker,
But winds come up from the shore,
They shake when the winds roar,
Old bones upon the mountain shake.'

All those around him knew that Yeats's time was short. But they did not know how short. His doctor told George that her husband might live another six months. But two or three days after that, his body gave him notice.

His breathing became difficult and he was in great pain, which had to be dulled with morphia. He drifted in and out of delirium, for a while gained strength enough to dictate to George some final corrections to 'The Death of Cuchulain' and 'Under Ben Bulben', before a final relapse. He died on the afternoon of Saturday, 28 January, 1939.

Yeats had asked George that his body should remain in France for a year – he did not want an elaborate state funeral in Ireland – before being removed to Drumcliffe. Before the year was out, France and England were at war with Germany; Ireland had declared its neutrality. Yeats's body remained in the cemetery of Roquebrune, above the Mediterranean, until September 1948, when one of the ships of the small Irish navy came to bring it home. The state funeral happened, stage-managed by the son of Maud Gonne and John McBride, Sean McBride, now Ireland's Minister for External Affairs, and with President de Valera himself as the chief mourner.

The grave at Drumcliffe, with Yeats's epitaph incised upon the stone as he had ordained, became a place of controversy in 1986 when newspapers in England and Ireland published stories suggesting that the body laid to rest under Ben Bulben was not that of Yeats at all. It turned out that around 1944 the poet's remains had been transferred from the temporary burial place at Roquebrune to the cemetery's ossuary. This had been discovered by Edith Shackleton Heald in June 1947, when she had gone to see the grave, to find it was no longer there. She, with Yeats's friend the artist Edmund Dulac, arranged for a headstone to be placed in the cemetery, but when plans were announced to transfer the body to Ireland, Dulac informed George Yeats of the removal. Investigations were made, a set of bones was produced and attested as Yeats's, and accepted as such by the family. Michael Yeats, himself by 1986 an ex-Senator of the Irish Republic, strongly defended the authenticity of the Drumcliffe burial. Though doubts remain, the matter is basically unimportant. Yeats has his desired monument, where he wanted it to be, in the country-side that inspired him and which his own words have enriched; and where his shade can be fittingly honoured.

CHRONOLOGY

1865 Born on June 13 in Sandymount Avenue, Dublin.

1866 Birth of his sister Susan Mary (Lily).

1867 Removal of the family to London.

1868 Birth of his sister Elizabeth Corbet (Lolly). First of many summers in Sligo.

1870 Birth of his brother Robert Corbet (dies three years later).

1871 Birth of his brother John Butler (Jack).

1872 His mother goes with the children to Sligo.

1874 They move back to J.B. Yeats in London.

1875 Birth of his sister Jane Grace (dies the following year).

1877 Yeats starts at the Godolphin School, West London (until 1881).

1879 The family moves to Bedford Park, Chiswick, West London.

1881 The family moves back to Ireland, to a cottage at Howth. Yeats enrols at Erasmus Smith High School, Dublin.

1882 Yeats's friendship with Laura Armstrong begins.

1884 The family moves to Terenure. Yeats enrols at the Metropolitan School of Art, Dublin.

1885 First publication of his works, in *Dublin University Review*. He helps found the Dublin Hermetic Society.

1886 Yeats begins 'The Wanderings of Oisin', his first important poem.

1887 The family returns to London again. Yeats meets Madame Blavatsky.

1888 Yeats attends his first séance, and joins the Esoteric Section of the Theosophical Society. He is commissioned to write *Fairy and Folk Tales of the Irish Peasantry.*

1889 Yeats's first meeting with Maud Gonne (January 30). Publication of *The Wanderings of Oisin and Other Poems.* Yeats at work with Edwin Ellis on an annotated edition of William Blake's poems.

1890 Yeats helps found the Rhymers' Club in London. He is initiated into the Hermetic Order of the Golden Dawn, and is asked to leave the Esoteric section of the Theosophical Society.

1891 Foundation of the Irish Literary Society, in London and Dublin. Yeats publishes an anthology, *Representative Irish Tales,* the novella *John Sherman* and the story *Dhoya,* these under pseudonym 'Ganconagh'.

1892 Yeats fails to gain control of the Library of Ireland project. Publications include *Irish Fairy Tales,* and *The Countess Kathleen and Various Legends and Lyrics.* Stories being written at this time will be published in *The Secret Rose.*

1893 Publication of the William Blake edition (3 volumes), and *The Celtic Twilight.* Further 'Secret Rose' stories written.

1894 Yeats's first visit to Paris. London production of 'The Land of Heart's Desire', his first 'regular' play.

1895 Yeats visits Castle Rock in Lough Key and dreams of an Order of Celtic Mysteries. Birth of Iseult Gonne. He leaves the family house in London to live independently.

1896 Yeats meets Olivia Shakespear, who becomes his first mistress. He visits the Aran Islands and Paris, where he meets J.M. Synge.

1897 His first stay at Coole, with Lady Gregory, to be repeated annually for twenty years. Proposal drawn up for an Irish Literary Theatre. Publication of *The Secret Rose*.

1898 A further visit to Paris. Yeats learns about Maud Gonne's 'other life'.

1899 Publication of *The Wind Among the Reeds*. Yeats and George Moore collaborate on 'Diarmuid and Grania'.

1900 Yeats's mother dies. Disputes within the Golden Dawn Order. Publication of *The Shadowy Waters*.

1901 Production of 'Diarmuid and Grania'.

1902 Production of 'Cathleen ni Houlihan', starring Maud Gonne. The Yeats sisters move to Dublin with the founding of Dun Emer press. Yeats meets James Joyce.

1903 Formation of the Irish National Theatre Society, with Yeats as president. Maud Gonne marries John McBride. Yeats begins affair with Florence Farr. He makes his first American lecture tour. Publication of *In the Seven Woods*.

1904 'Where There is Nothing' produced at the Royal Court Theatre, London. Abbey Theatre opens (December).

1905 Maud Gonne is granted a legal separation from John McBride.

1906 'Deirdre' produced at the Abbey. Yeats publishes his selection of Spenser's poems, also his own *Collected Poems*.

1907 Riots at the Abbey on performance of 'The Playboy of the Western World'. Yeats visits Italy with Lady Gregory and her son. His father moves to live in New York.

1908 Yeats's affair with Mabel Dickinson begins.

1909 Yeats applies for a post at University College, Dublin.

1910 Yeats accepts a pension from the British gov-
      ernment. Publication of *The Green Helmet and
      Other Poems*.

1911 Yeats revisits Paris. First American tour of the
      Abbey company generates controversy.

1912 Abbey players briefly arrested in Philadel-
      phia. Yeats meet Rabindranath Tagore. He
      visits Maud Gonne in Normandy.

1913 Yeats joins the Society for Psychical Re-
      search. Yeats and Ezra Pound work together
      in Sussex during the winter. Break-up of
      the affair with Mabel Dickinson. He meets
      Georgie Hyde-Lees for the first time.

1914 Yeats goes on a US lecture tour, February-
      April. Publication of *Responsibilities.*

1915 Yeats spends January-February at Stone Cot-
      tage with Ezra Pound. Hugh Lane is drowned
      in the sinking of the *Lusitania* in May.
      Yeats tells his sister he has refused a knight-
      hood.

1916 Yeats's first 'Noh' drama, 'At the Hawk's Well',
      performed in London. The Easter Rising;
      Yeats proposes to Maud Gonne McBride,

now a widow. Publication of *Reveries Over Childhood and Youth*.

1917 Yeats purchases Thoor Ballylee. He proposes to Maud Gonne again; then to Iseult, finally to Georgie Hyde-Lees, who accepts. They are married on October 20. Start of the 'automatic writing' sessions, which go on until March 1920. Publication of *The Wild Swans at Coole*.

1918 Death of Robert Gregory. Publication of *Per Amica Silentia Lunae*. Maud Gonne enters Ireland illegally but Yeats refuses to let her into her house.

1919 Birth of Yeats's daughter Anne (February). 'The Player Queen' performed in London and Dublin. Yeats gives up his Woburn Buildings lodgings; they move to Oxford.

1920 Yeats does another North American lecture tour. From automatic writing he and his wife switch to 'sleep sessions'.

1921 Birth of Yeats's son Michael (August). The Yeatses rent a house at Thame, near Oxford. 'Four Plays for Dancers' completes his set of 'Noh' dramas.

1922 Death of Yeats's father, in New York. The fam-
      ily move to Merrion Square, Dublin. Yeats
      receives honorary doctorates in Belfast and
      Dublin, and is appointed to the Senate.

1923 Yeats is awarded the Nobel Prize for Literature.

1924 Publication of Yeats's *Essays*.

1925 Yeats revisits Italy. He makes his most famous
      Senate speech, against the banning of divorce
      in Ireland.

1926 Publication of the first edition of *A Vision*. Ri-
      ots in the Abbey Theatre on performance of
      O'Casey's 'The Plough and the Stars'. Yeats
      chairs Senate committee on coinage de-
      sign. Publication of *Autobiographies*.

1927 Assassination of O'Higgins. A year of illness for
      Yeats, with winter visit to Spain and Southern
      France.

1928 Publication of *The Tower*. Controversy over
      the rejection of O'Casey's 'The Silver Tas-
      sie'. Yeats's term in the Senate ends. The fam-
      ily move from Merrion Square to Fitzwilliam
      Square. Winter at Rapallo with the Pounds.

1929 Yeats's first visit to Rome. Last summer at Ballylee. Winter in Rapallo. He makes his will, in anticipation of imminent death. Publication of *A Packet for Ezra Pound*.

1930 Censorship officially established in Ireland. Premiere of his play about Swift, 'The Words Upon the Window-Pane'.

1931 Publication of his last prose fiction, *Michael Robartes and His Friends*. Yeats spends much time at Coole with the ill Lady Gregory.

1932 Death of Lady Gregory. The Yeats family move out of Dublin to Rathfarnham. Irish Academy of Letters established, September. Yeats embarks on a US lecture tour, October – January.

1933 Dispute with the government over Abbey Theatre funding. Publication of *The Winding Stair* and *Collected Poems*.

1934 Yeats undergoes a rejuvenating operation. His affair with Margot Ruddock begins. Publication of *Collected Plays*.

1935 Yeats meets Lady Dorothy Wellesley. He spends the winter in Majorca with Shri Purohit Swami, translating *The Upanishads*.

1936 Yeats falls ill on Majorca. Publication of *The Oxford Book of Modern Verse, 1892–1935,* and *Dramatis Personae,* his final volume of autobiography.

1937 Yeats's affair with Edith Shackleton Heald begins. The second edition of *A Vision* is published, also *The Ten Principal Upanishads.*

1938 Death of Olivia Shakespear. Premiere of 'Purgatory' at the Abbey; publication of *New Poems.*

1939 Yeats dies at Roquebrune, France, January 28. Posthumous publication of *Last Poems and Two Plays,* and *On the Boiler.*

1948 Removal of Yeats's remains from France to Drumcliffe.

$\mathcal{A}$ SHORT LIST OF BOOKS ON YEATS

Yeats, William Butler: *The Poems, A New Edition,* edited by R. J. Finneran, London, 1984

The Poems, edited by Daniel Albright, revised edition, London, 1994

Memoirs, London, 1988

Autobiographies, London, 1955

The Letters of W.B. Yeats, edited by Allan Wade, London, 1954. (The complete letters are in process of publication by Oxford University Press)

Ellmann, Richard: *Yeats: The Man and the Masks,* revised edition, London, 1977

Jeffares, A. Norman: *W.B. Yeats: A New Biography,* London, 1986

Maddox, Brenda: *George's Ghosts: A New Life of W.B. Yeats,* London, 1995

Webster, B.: *Yeats: A Psychoanalytical Study, London, 1973*

There are very many books on Yeats, critical and biographical. Suggestive chapters or comments on Yeats are also to be found in many general works, including two important works of poetic criticism published in his lifetime: *Axel's Castle* by Edmund Wilson (New York, 1931); and *Seven Types of Ambiguity* by William Empson (London, 1930).